ROMAN JAKOBSON'S
APPROACH
TO LANGUAGE

ROMAN JAKOBSON'S APPROACH TO LANGUAGE

Phenomenological Structuralism

Elmar Holenstein

*Translated by Catherine Schelbert
and Tarcisius Schelbert*

INDIANA UNIVERSITY PRESS
Bloomington & London

Daně
oddaně

Originally published as *Jakobson ou le structuralisme phénoménologique*
© 1974 by Éditions Seghers-Paris

English translation copyright © 1976 by Indiana University Press

Published in Canada by Fitzhenry & Whiteside Limited, Don Mills, Ontario

Manufactured in the United States of America

Library of Congress Cataloging in Publication Data

Holenstein, Elmar.
    Roman Jakobson's approach to language.

    Translation of Roman Jakobsons phänomenologischer Strukturalismus.
    Originally presented as the author's Habilitationsschrift, Zürich, 1974.
    Bibliography
    Includes indexes.
    1. Jakobson, Roman, 1896-   2. Structural
linguistics. 3. Languages—Philosophy. I. Title.
P85.J3H613 1976   301.2'1   76-12368
ISBN 0-253-35018-2   1 2 3 4 5 80 79 78 77 76

CONTENTS

v

2. Philosophical and Methodological Principles

Acknowledgment

The research underlying this book was made possible by a generous grant from the *Schweizerische Geisteswissenschaftliche Gesellschaft.*

I am particularly indebted to Professor Roman Jakobson. While doing research in Cambridge, Mass., in the spring of 1973, I was able to spend many hours with him, during which he familiarized me with the history, topics, and goals of structural linguistics. He subsequently sent me many suggestions for corrections and additions to a first draft of the German text and later to the French edition as well. I can only hope that Professor Jakobson's generous support and encouragement will in turn prove fruitful for his imposing lifework.

ELMAR HOLENSTEIN

1.

Introduction

1.1. *Phenomenological structuralism*

Were we to comprise the leading idea of present-day science in its most various manifestations, we could hardly find a more appropriate designation than *structuralism*. Any set of phenomena examined by contemporary science is treated not as a mechanical agglomeration but as a structural whole, and the basic task is to reveal the inner, whether static or developmental, laws of this system. What appears to be the focus of scientific preoccupations is no longer the outer stimulus, but the internal premises of the development; now the mechanical conception of processes yields to the question of their functions. (1929b:SW II 711)

Were we to characterize the work of the man who wrote these lines forty-five years ago in the Prague weekly *Čin* ["Action"], thus coining the key word for an interdisciplinary scientific movement of international proportions, we could hardly find a more appropriate designation than *phenomenological structuralism*.

At first glance this designation may appear to be an oxymoron, quite like speaking of a wooden iron. Proponents of both phenomenology and structuralism have found the approach and procedure of the two movements incompatible. And indeed, their offshoots have developed in diametrically opposed directions: on the phenomenological side toward a cloudy irrationalism, on the structuralistic side toward an exclusively descriptive and positivistic formalism.

A look at the beginnings of phenomenology and the East European branch of structuralism reveals an entirely different picture. The two fields soon prove to have many points in common, both historically and materially. Let us begin with the key idea that Jakobson brought forward in 1929 as characteristic of the new sciences. It was in Husserl's work that Jakobson found the first systematic formulation of the general laws that are operative for a structural unit. In the third Logical Investigation (1913), entitled "On the theory of wholes and parts," Husserl treats precisely those laws that are constitutive of a system, a unified whole. On the occasion of the second edition of the *Logical Investigations,* Husserl (1913:49) expressed his regret and incomprehension that the third investigation had met with little recognition. As late as 1928, he still recommended it to his students as the best introduction to the study of phenomenological philosophy (Spiegelberg, 1971:78). Yet history would have it that this very investigation, which found hardly an echo among Husserl's own students, was seized upon by the Prague linguists without his knowledge and proclaimed a kind of "fundamental view of structuralism" by Jakobson. For his trailblazing study on child language (1941:SW I 328), Jakobson chose the first motto from this part of the *Logical Investigations* (1913:478): "The only true unifying factors are the relations of foundedness (*Fundierung*)."

Moreover, several of Husserl's students were active in the *Cercle linguistique de Prague* (Landgrebe, Pos, Čiževskij). Husserl himself, on Jakobson's initiative, presented a lecture to the *Cercle* in 1935 on the phenomenology of language.

Husserl's influence is most tangible in Jakobson's work

(Holenstein, 1973). A consideration of explicit quotations yields three principal themes in which Husserl's influence can be directly observed: the determination of the relationship between linguistics and psychology, the program for a "universal grammar," and the defense of semantics as an integral part of linguistics. But the affinity goes much farther and deeper. The following discussion will show that there is hardly a basic theoretical and methodological concept of structural linguistics and poetics that does not undergo an explicit or implicit phenomenological determination and elaboration by Jakobson. It was above all the historic change of course, the supersession by a phenomenological attitude of the naturalism which dominated philosophy and scientific methodology at the turn of the century, that gave the initial impetus for shifting the proper weight to the structural approach. In this sense, phenomenology represents the historical and logical "condition of possibility" of structuralism.

> When the rise of the phenomenological orientation to a top ranking position in the scientific system began to displace the naturalistic approach, linguistics reflected this trend by an active, growing interest in the problems of the language system, the inner structure of language, and the relationship between the different levels of language. A theoretically elucidated doctrine of form became the order of the day, the focus shifted to the question of the relationship between form and function, and even in sound theory the conception of the natural sciences had to yield step by step to the analysis of the linguistic function. Correspondingly, the question of the inner laws of linguistic change was given precedence in historical linguistics. (1936c:81)

The comparison of structuralism and phenomenology can commence with Husserl's division of phenomenology into four partially overlapping departments—static, genetic, eidetic, and transcendental.

Static phenomenology involves the delineation of the set of structural types inherent to individual objects. Two types of structures are preëminent for Husserl, the relations of foundedness operative for the different aspects of an object, and the relation of the object to the subject by which it is intended. In Husserl's presentation of the relations of foundedness, Jakobson saw, as we have said above, the first fundamental formulation of the concern of the structural sciences. In Prague structuralism, the relation of objects to subject plays a lesser role only *de facto* and not *de jure*. The leading collaborators of the *Cercle* were linguists, not psychologists.

Phenomenology and structuralism both launched their exemplary researches with the elucidation of static structures. Their holistic analyses were designed to counteract the mechanistic-causal, pointillistic explanation of isolated facts prevalent toward the end of the nineteenth century. This new kind of explanation was held to be the only scientific form of genetic explanation. It is worthy of note that both phenomenology and structuralism included problems of development in their programs upon independently discovering forms of genesis other than mechanistic-causal ones. In Husserl's case it was motivation, a specific form of causality that links up not physicalistic, but psychical and mental data. This was for Husserl the subject matter of *genetic phenomenology*. For Jakobson it was function, a teleological criterion, which was recognized as decisive for the development of language.

Eidetic phenomenology is concerned with the grasp of the essential features common to objects of the same category. The search for the invariants in manifold variations is the program that structural linguistics shares with all modern sciences. Although the ontological status of invariants and the epistemological problem of their extraction do not concern structuralism as much as they do phenomenology, they are certainly not absent. The specific contribution of structuralism to eidetic phenomenology lies in the elaboration of the relational and hierarchical character of essential features.

The last place one might expect common ground is between structuralism and *transcendental phenomenology*. Should one, however, succeed in breaking the traditional bonds of transcendental philosophy, highly stimulating points of contact emerge. Negatively formulated, the concern of transcendental phenomenology appears as a reduction. The physicalistic explanation for any and every form of world-experience is ruled out. Positively formulated, all data are elucidated according as their structure and sense (function) appear to a subject. Traditional transcendental philosophers, including Husserl, organized the data of the world largely in psychological terms. Structuralism offers the tools and material for a semiotic apprehension of the transcendental approach. Transcendental philosophy proceeds from the observation that all consciousness is a "consciousness of something" and that the world can in principle be given to us only in a subjective mode of appearance as a perceived, remembered, imagined, thought, or otherwise conscious world. Structuralism draws our attention to the root-like attachment of the world's subjective constitution to sign systems.

These manifold affinities, which touch the core of both movements, will receive more detailed attention later. They must not, however, obscure the differences that nevertheless exist between Jakobson's structuralism and Husserl's phenomenology. The most important point is that Jakobson did not concur with the methodological monism to which phenomenology increasingly fell victim. The nature of phenomena, which is the concern of structural linguistics, obviously allows for a fruitful application of the methods, rebuffed by phenomenology, of empirical induction and mathematical formalization. Here, a second basic trait of Jakobson's structuralism emerges, namely, its integral character.

1.2. *Integral linguistics*

It is characteristic of Jakobson's linguistics that it embraces all aspects, levels, and related points of language and takes into account both their inner autonomy and their interdependence. Reductions, or to use a more linguistic expression, excommunications, are foreign to it. Meaning is not excluded to the sole advantage of syntax, diachrony to that of synchrony, everyday language to that of the formalized languages of the exact sciences, inner language to that of the externally observable language of intersubjective communication. This is what distinguishes Jakobson's structural linguistics from the American structuralism of the post-Bloomfieldian era, from the French structuralism of Saussurian bent, and from the analytical language philosophies that followed in the wake of Carnap and Wittgenstein.

Intralinguistic integration is combined with interdisciplinary integration. Linguistics is not isolated from the natural sciences (biology, physiology, etc.) or from other formal sciences (logic, mathematics), nor is it absorbed by them. There is with Jakobson no precipitate identification of linguistic and neurological factors or of language and thought. In the conventional treatment of the problems presented here, two types of solutions dominate. According to the first, linguistic facts L_1, L_2, L_3, ..., L_n are causally attributed to individual psychological or physiological facts P_1, P_2, P_3, ..., P_n. Thus, about a century ago, an attempt was made to derive sound shifts from changes in the speech organs, changes explained in turn by external influences of an ecological or sociological nature. Isomorphic solutions predominate today. The system of rules $L_1 - L_2 - L_3 - - -$ L_n of a language is seen as the mirror image of an innate neurological system of rules $P_1 - P_2 - P_3 - - - P_n$. Jakobson's approach shows more affinity with the second, holistic type of solution than with the first atomistic type. Besides the simple relationship of isomorphism, however, he considers more complex forms of correlation as well. The transition from one system to another does not necessarily consist of a simple shift of structure to another substance, but often of a kind of structural transformation to be further defined. (See Figure 1.)

> Characteristic of the basic and unique trend of current Russian science* is that the correlativity between single series is not

*Jakobson refers in particular to the geography of V. V. Dokučajev, who was

thought in causal terms, the one series is not derived from the other; the basic picture with which science operates is a system of correlative series, a structure to be viewed immanently and endowed with its own inner laws. (1929d:633)

The explanation of a linguistic fact involves two stages, a purely linguistic and an interdisciplinary one. In the first stage, the linguistic fact under consideration, L_1, is not directly explained in terms of a psychological or neurological fact P_1, as in the old school of psychologistic linguistics; it is rather investigated in terms of its relation to the other linguistic facts from L_2 to L_n. In the second, interdisciplinary stage, the system of all linguistic facts is placed in relation to the systems of the other sciences.

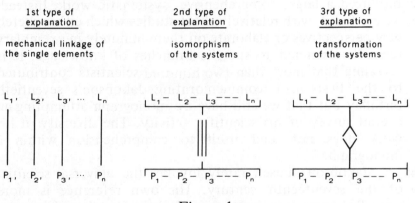

1st type of explanation	2nd type of explanation	3rd type of explanation
mechanical linkage of the single elements	isomorphism of the systems	transformation of the systems

Figure 1

Structuralism, as Jakobson understands it, leads to a general science whose object can be designated as the all-inclusive system of all individual systems, "the system of

brought to his notice by a Russian professor in Prague, the geographer and scholar P. N. Savickij (see CLP, 1931a:300). These Russian geographers are important forerunners of contemporary ecology (Odum, 1971:9). The impulse given by geography to the application of structural methods is further remarkable in view of the fact that Lévi-Strauss finds another earth science, geology, a source of great inspiration. The multidimensional, interdisciplinary approach is, however, much more evident in geography and ecology than in geology.

systems," as Jakobson himself formulated it in a programmatic text written with Tynjanov in 1928 (386ff.). This
theoretical platform as well as the active commitment to
interdisciplinary cooperation have been set forth in numerous
publications with collaborators from other sciences, and are
manifested in the increasing role of linguistics in the concert
of sciences. One is reminded of Leibniz, of his interdisciplinary activities and his program for a *mathesis uni-
versalis,* a "general science" in which a systematic place is
assigned to each of the sciences. The work of both scholars is
typified by an incredible wealth of extraordinarily diversified
research. Jakobson's investigations range from folkloric field
research in the environs of Moscow to sound analyses carried
out with the latest technical refinements at the laboratories
of the Massachusetts Institute of Technology. Neither man
produced a large, comprehensive, systematic work. Instead,
we are faced with relatively short studies which either sketch
new perspectives or elaborate on them minutely in exemplary
research restricted to specific branches of knowledge. It is
revealing that more than two hundred scientists contributed
to the Festschrift commemorating Jakobson's seventieth
birthday but that we still have no monograph attempting an
overall survey of his scientific activity. The diversity of his
work does not lend itself to comprehension within a
monograph.

Jakobson himself rarely invokes the universal scientist
of the seventeenth century. His own reference is more
appealing, more humane, more linguistic. He takes pleasure in
paraphrasing Terence's saying as *Linguista sum; linguistici
nihil a me alienum puto* ("I am a linguist. I know of nothing
linguistic that is foreign to me") (1953b:SW II 555).*

1.3. *The stages in Jakobson's scientific career*

1.3.1. *Moscow.* In 1915, the nineteen-year-old Jakobson
with six other students founded the "Moscow Linguistic

*The first to paraphrase Terence with these words seems to have been L.
Tesnière (CLP, 1931b:309).

Circle" (*Moskovskij lingvističeskij kruzok*). Its aim was "the study of linguistics, poetics, metrics, and folklore" (1965c:SW II 530). The group soon attracted all the younger linguists in Moscow as well as philosophers such as Husserl's student, Gustav Špet, and even poets, Majakovskij in particular. Together with a similar circle in Petersburg, *OPOJAZ*, the Moscow Circle has gone down in the history of literature under the heading of Russian formalism. It repudiated the nineteenth century biographical and cultural interpretation of literature and the symbolist conception of the poet as an inspired vehicle of wisdom. Viewing the poet as a craftsman, the Circle worked at defining the devices he used in his craftsmanship. The best-known device described by the formalists is deformation or *estrangement*. A linguistic conception of the study of literature is especially typical of the Moscow Circle. Later Jakobson firmly rejected certain basic principles of formalism, such as the construction of irreconcilable antinomies (literary vs. social factors, medium vs. the reference of language, etc.), and also erroneous interpretations of deformation as a poetic device (1935b; 1965d). On the other hand, essential traits of Prague structuralism are clearly anchored in Russian formalism, e.g., ideas adopted from cubism and futurism, which resulted in the concept of a dynamic interrelation of different perspectives and aspects and in the thesis of the creativity of language (1919:25ff.).

1.3.2. *Prague and Brno.* Upon moving to Czechoslovakia, Jakobson played a major role in the foundation of the *Cercle linguistique de Prague* in 1926. The new Circle fast became the most active and creative promotor and propagator of structural and functional linguistics during the interwar period. Besides Jakobson, the Czechs Mathesius, Havránek, and Mukařovský, and the Russians Trubetzkoy, Bogatyrev, and Karcevskij counted among the more prominent members. Research centered on phonology, morphology, poetics, and the history of Slavic languages and literatures. The principal characteristic of Prague structuralism is its bridging of the antinomies outlined by both Russian formalism and Saussure's new language theory. Jakobson, in his pioneering works on the history of sounds in Russian (1928a; 1929a), demonstrates that the same structural and functional laws that are constitutive of a synchronic system also apply to diachronic development, and that synchrony and diachrony form an inseparable dynamic unit.

Brno, where Jakobson began teaching at the Masaryk University in 1933, can be considered a separate station in his research activity, since it was during his last years there that he developed the theory of distinctive features with which he advanced significantly beyond the classical phonology of the Prague Circle, as recorded in Trubetzkoy's 1939 *Grundzüge der Phonologie* ("Principles of Phonology").

1.3.3. *Scandinavia.* The Nazi occupation of Czechoslovakia (1939) drove Jakobson to Denmark and Norway. The occupation of Norway and the threatening successes of the German army forced him to further flight, first to Sweden (1940) and then to the United States (1941). During the intermezzo in Scandinavia, Jakobson tackled the first phase of his investigation of child language and aphasia.

1.3.4. *New York and Cambridge, Mass.* In the United States, Jakobson initially taught at Columbia University and at the Franco-Belgian Institute in New York, the *Ecole Libre des Hautes Etudes.* Since 1949 he has been at Harvard University, and he was the first scientist to receive, in 1957, a second chair as Institute Professor at neighboring M.I.T. It was in the earliest New York years that Jakobson first met Lévi-Strauss. Through him and Lacan, Jakobson was to exercise a major influence on the course of French structuralism. Often quoted is Lévi-Strauss's remark about his colleague, that he had found in him a scholar who "has not only raised the same problems but has already solved them as well" (Pingaud, 1965:4). Aided by the professional and technical resources at his disposal in Cambridge, Jakobson provided his phonological theory with a well-balanced conclusion and also furnished it with a broader foundation through his collaboration with scientists in acoustics (spectral analysis) and cybernetics (communication theory).

American linguistics underwent a profound upheaval

toward the end of the fifties. Neorationalistic conceptions wreaked havoc with the empirical and behavioristic underpinnings of Bloomfieldian linguistics. Jakobson had no small share in this new orientation. The most eminent proponent of transformational grammar, Noam Chomsky, was his student at Harvard and is now his colleague at M.I.T. The same is true of Morris Halle, the initiator of generative phonology. However, Chomsky's critique of post-Bloomfieldian linguistics, which he usually presents as a critique of structuralism, has led to confusion. It is easy to forget that the term structuralism has been applied to both post-Bloomfieldian linguistics in the United States and the linguistics of Saussure and the Prague Circle in Europe. To preclude misunderstandings, an explicit comment by Chomsky (1972b:64) is cited here (see also section 2.4.): "Personally, I have learned a great deal from European structuralism, especially from my professor and close friend, Roman Jakobson. I do not have to call to mind how essential his contributions have remained."

To draw a somewhat simplified picture of Jakobson's career, one might designate the Moscow period as the phase of stormy departure, the Prague period as the constructive phase with, on the one hand, the delineation of a systematic program and, on the other, the testing of this program through investigations of distinct, narrow fields of research, and the American period as the phase of interdisciplinary consolidation and expansion of insights already attained.

The Moscow and Prague years were characterized by close contact with writers and artists. The best known in Moscow were Xlebnikov, Majakovskij, Mandel'štam, and Pasternak, and in Prague writers Nezval, Seifert, and Vančura, and artists Teige and Šima (1972c:38ff.). Jakobson did not lose touch after the Second World War. He maintained contact also with the French writers Louis Aragon and Elsa Triolet, who had been his friend since his Moscow days. However, in America, Jakobson has devoted himself more and more to interdisciplinary scientific collaboration with such diverse researchers as topologist W. Hurewicz, physicist

Niels Bohr, biologists such as F. Jacob and the scientists of
the Salk Institute, neurologist and expert on aphasia A. R.
Luria, physiologist G. von Békésy, psychologists Jerome S.
Bruner and S. S. Stevens, the founders of cybernetics and
information theory Norbert Wiener, E. Colin Cherry, D.
Gabor, and D. M. MacKay, and many others.

In philosophical questions, Husserl dominated the field
in Moscow and Prague, although there were certainly other
philosophers. In both Russia and Czechoslovakia there was a
strong Hegelian tradition (1933:SW II 543; Tschižewskij,
1961). Significantly, an American philosopher, Charles
Sanders Peirce, became increasingly influential after the
Second World War, perhaps even replacing Husserl. Jakobson
(1971b:SW II, p. v) called him "the most powerful source of
information" that he had found in the United States. The
personal contact with analytic philosophers, with Carnap in
Prague and Quine at Harvard, also deserves mention (Jakobson, 1965c:SW II 534; Quine, 1960:138).

1.4. *Structuralistic trends at the start of the twentieth century*

At the turn of the century, structuralistic tendencies
surfaced in different places and in diverse fields of scholarship. A brief survey will show the influence of these trends
on Jakobson's structuralism and will demonstrate the originality of his thought against this background.

1.4.1. *The distinction between the genetic and descriptive
methods in the Brentano school.* In contrast to the predominant genetic approach of most scientific endeavor in the
second half of the nineteenth century, the Viennese philosopher Franz Brentano was committed to a fundamental
distinction between the genetic and descriptive methods
within psychology. Genetic psychology explains psychical
data in terms of other, preceding psychical events and, in the
last analysis, of physiological processes, which are in turn
thought to be released by the surrounding physical processes
in nature. Its method is that of mechanistic-causal explana-

tion. Descriptive psychology, on the other hand, seeks to uncover the inherent relations characterizing the various data of experience. Its method is that of descriptive classification. It is based not on induction, but on the intuition of the object. Brentano opposed, for instance, the genetic explanation of a judgment as arising out of an inseparably fixed association of ideas. According to Brentano (1925:202ff., 224f.), the associative-theoretical explanation confuses that which can be considered the cause of the judgment, namely that among two properties it is impossible to think the one without the other, with the specific property of the judgment, which Brentano sees as the belief or affirmation of a combination of properties.

The same genetic approach applied in psychology also dominated linguistics. In the words of Hermann Paul (1889:XLVI): "It has been objected that there is another view of language possible besides the historical. I must contradict this." Two of Brentano's students teaching in Prague were among the opponents of Paul, Thomas Masaryk (1887:191), who was to become president of the Czechoslovakian Republic and patron of the *Cercle linguistique de Prague,* and Anton Marty (1908:34ff.). Through their efforts and those of two still more prominent students, Carl Stumpf and Edmund Husserl, Brentano's methodological distinction was to exercise a major influence on the Prague structuralists. In Saussure's thought, synchrony and diachrony stand in brusque and irreconcilable opposition to each other. The Brentano school, however, is primarily concerned with the methodological precedence of static over genetic aspects. What is decisive is the insight that the genesis and development of language cannot be approached relevantly until its "essence" has first been elucidated (Jakobson, 1930a:SW II 471ff.; 1933:SW II 543).

In this connection, Stumpf (1907:28ff.; 61ff.*), fol-

*There are no references indicating that the Prague structuralists were familiar with this theoretical treatise by Stumpf. His studies on the perception of color and sound, however, belonged to their basic literature (see Jakobson, 1919:26; 1941:SW I 378ff.).

lowing Dilthey (1894:176), speaks explicitly of "structural laws." He predicted a trend toward a "transformation of our mechanical Weltanschauung into more abstract forms," in which excessive concentration on the causal laws of succession would be supplemented by the elaboration of structural laws immanent in the different spheres of appearance. Their theme is the ordered coexistence of the parts of a whole. They can be mathematically defined, thus making it possible to apply algebraic operations to qualitatives.

1.4.2. *Titchener's structural psychology.* In Edward B. Titchener's program for a structural psychology (1898), the structural description is not opposed to the genetic-causal explanation, as in the Brentano school, but rather to the functional explanation. Mentioning the division of biology into anatomy (morphology) and physiology, Titchener advocates an analogous division of psychology into a structural and a functional discipline. Methodologically, the first precedes the second. Its task is to dissect and isolate the components and elementary processes upon which a datum builds, as well as to describe the properties of these elementary components. As functional constructions, the higher-level, meaning-implicating processes such as apperception and judgment are reduced by structural psychology to the elementary processes of sensation and affection.

The term *structural* can be construed in two ways. An approach may be called structural when it aims at either the elements of which a formation is put together or the relations between the parts of a whole. Titchener's structural psychology is obviously closer to an atomistic theory of construction than to a theory of relations. Because of this and because of its antifunctionalist attitude, it stands in harsh contrast to the structuralism of Jakobson and of the Prague Circle. The so-called American structuralism of Bloomfieldian linguistics, on the other hand, with its taxonomic,* afunc-

*Following biology, in which taxonomy, as the classification of the species, corresponds to the morphology of the individual, Titchener treats structural and taxonomic psychology on the same level. The former deals with the specification of components of individual conscious; the latter with the classification of the psychical characteristics of social classes.

tional tendency to ignore meaning, shows more affinity with
Titchener's line of thought, with the exception of his
mentalistic commitments. The Prague structuralists combined
the structural and functional approach to language from the
start. Vilém Mathesius entitled the paper in which he
informed the Second International Congress of Linguists in
Geneva, 1931, about the work underway in Prague, "*La place
de la linguistique fonctionelle et structurale dans le développement des études linguistiques.*"* Actually, the basic concepts of the Prague Circle, such as the phoneme and binary
opposition, are only to be understood functionally. A
phonological variation is distinguished from an ordinary
phonetic variation by its function of differentiating meaning.
Binary opposition, as confirmed by communication theory, is
the most efficient and economic means of conveying information, i.e., of the reduction of an in- or overdetermination.

In their functional analysis, the Prague structuralists
profited especially from the teachings of the Polish linguist
Jan Baudouin de Courtenay, a pioneer in the theory of the
phoneme, and from Marty, whose lectures at the German
University in Prague were attended by Mathesius. Marty
(1875) traced the origin of language to what he considered a
conscious but planless objective, namely the intention of
intersubjective communication. The Prague structuralists
adopted his teleological concept of language as a means of
communication but rejected the characterization of its
fundamental intention as a planless and (consistently) conscious objective.

Mathesius had emphasized structure and function; two
years later, Trubetzkoy (1933) singled out structuralism and
universalism as the characteristics distinguishing the new
phonology from the atomizing and individualizing approach
of scientific research around 1900. The atomistic isolation of
elements gave way to a structural investigation of the relation
between the parts of a system, and the orientation toward

*Cf. Mathesius' programmatic opening address at the First Congress of Slavic
Philologists, 1929 (see Jakobson, 1930b:387) and at the International Phonological Congress, 1930 (Mathesius, 1931a:291), both in Prague.

individual multiplicities of linguistic phenomena yielded to a concentration on the universal and invariant traits of language basic to subjective communication.

The Prague Circle shares this antiatomistic, holistic attitude with a third structuralistic trend, gestalt psychology. 1.4.3. *Gestalt psychology*. The main accent of gestalt theory lies in the opposition of atom or element and structure or gestalt, not in the opposition of causal or functional and intrinsically structural relations immanent in the object as such. The very structure becomes the focus of research.

Gestalt psychology primarily disputes the self-contradictory and unreflected assumption of atomistic and amorphous sense data whose mechanically occurring accumulation was alleged to produce the meaningful constructs of experience and thought. The thesis of gestalt psychology is that even the simplest data of perception display a necessary, constitutive network of relations, which is no external happenstance. Moreover, the natural parts into which a perception can be dissected are already structured. Like the total perception, they too have a holistic character. Therefore, gestalt psychology speaks of "partial wholes" (*Teilganze*). Jakobson (1931a:SW I 202) was to apply this concept to phonology. A sense datum can appear only on a background with whose qualitative nature its own nature varies, in other words, with which it forms a whole. The influence of the whole on its parts is strongest when it forms a so-called good gestalt, i.e., when it is qualified by a particularly excellent property. The *dynamic* aspect of gestalt theory, the thesis that every datum is determined by its field, rests on this observation.

A whole has properties that its parts, taken individually, do not have. Harmony and rhythm are properties of a sequence of notes but never of an isolated note. On this observation rests the *static* or formal aspect of gestalt theory, the thesis that the whole is more than the sum of its parts.

The transsummative qualities of a gestalt (*Übersummativität*) can be transferred to entirely different multiplicities of elements without affecting the gestalt quality. It remains invariant as opposed to its variable parts. On this observation rests the *universal* aspect of gestalt theory, the thesis of the transposability of gestalts.

The characteristics of field dependence, transsummativity, and transposability or universality also hold for the relation of opposition, which plays such a basic role in the build-up of language. In Danish, for example, the strong and weak opposition of [t] vs. [d] in a strong position is transferred to [d] vs. [ð] in a weak position. The weak phoneme in the strong position coincides materially with the strong phoneme in the weak position. This does not affect the formal opposition between strong and weak as a gestalt quality and basic criterion of perception. In discussing transposable relations in sound perception, Jakobson points out that Köhler made analogous observations with animals.

> In W. Köhler's experiment, chickens were trained to pick grain from a gray field and to leave the grain untouched on the adjacent darker field; when the pair of fields, gray and dark, was later replaced by a pair, gray and light, the chickens looking for their food left the gray field for its lighter counterpart. Thus "the chicken transfers its response to the relatively brighter area." (1956a:SW I 473)

Invariance applies not only within a single language (intralingual) but also across different languages (interlingual).

> A pair of palatal vowel phonemes, genetically opposed to each other by relative wideness and narrowness and, acoustically, by a higher and lower concentration of energy (compact/diffuse), may in some languages be implemented in one position as [æ] − [e] and in another position as [e] − [i], so that the same sound [e] in one position implements the diffuse, and in another, the compact term of the same opposition. The relation in both positions remains identical. (ibid.)

The East European linguists maintained close contact with gestalt theory. As a student at the University of

Moscow, Jakobson participated in 1915/16 in a psychology seminar on Kurt Koffka (1912). In Prague he made the acquaintance of Christian von Ehrenfels, who was teaching at the German University there. Ehrenfels, with his paper (1890) on the transsummativity and transposability of gestalt qualities, had launched the movement of gestalt theory. When Jakobson, during his Prague years (1931a:SW I 202) speaks of "modern psychology," he means gestalt psychology.

However, the divergences between Prague structuralism and gestalt psychology cannot be ignored. (1) Structuralism replaces the relatively vague concept of field by the concept of a hierarchically structured system. (2) In gestalt psychology, properties such as simplicity, symmetry, balance, and closedness dominate as gestalt qualities, while the main concern of structuralism in this respect is binary opposition. (3) Gestalt psychology with its primarily static orientation neglects the genetic and, up to Kurt Lewin's (1926) revolutionizing experiments, the functional perspective as well, whereas the Prague Circle allotted a dominant position to the dynamic, genetic, and functional aspects in their researches from the start. (4) In the sphere of language, the structuralists, orienting themselves according to specific linguistic criteria, were able to uncover connections overlooked by the gestaltists with their very general criteria extracted from the psychology of perception. This applies especially to the build-up of the phonological system and the phenomena of aphasia. In his investigations, Jakobson made significant advances beyond the analyses of Köhler (and Stumpf) in the theory of sounds (1941:SW I 378ff.) and the findings of Kurt Goldstein in speech disorders (1956b:SW II 245ff.).

1.4.4. *Saussure's concept of a general theory of language.* It is to Ferdinand de Saussure that we owe the first explicit, comprehensive, and specifically linguistic formulation of a theory of language. Although one can certainly find forerunners for each of his ideas, Saussure did not simply let the matter rest with the flashes of inspiration of preceding decades and even centuries. He worked these ideas into a systematic and therefore fruitful theory, as a result of which he has come, especially in French-speaking areas, to be called the father of structuralism.

The relationship of the East Europeans to Saussure is more complex. One could compare his position with that of an older step-brother. The parent common to both is the Kazan school of linguistics, represented by the above-mentioned Baudouin de Courtenay and his philosophically talented student and co-worker, Mikołaj Kruszewski (Jakobson, 1960a:SW II 394ff.; 1965a:SW II 429ff.; De Mauro, 1972:339f.). We have these two to thank for an important contribution to the systematic and functional definition of the concept of the phoneme. In addition, Kruszewski was the first to work out the theory of the two axes of language, the syntagmatic and the paradigmatic axes, as they came to be called. Most of Saussure's famous conceptual pairs and dichotomies are to be found also in the work of the two Polish theorists of language.

The other parent of the Prague structuralists is the Brentano school. Husserl's *Logical Investigations* (1913), with the first investigation on "Expression and Meaning" containing the triadic division of the functions of linguistic expressions into meaning, reference, and intimation (emotive function) and with the fourth investigation on an autonomous theory of the forms of linguistic entities, the "universal grammar," were already known to Jakobson in 1915, two years before Sergej Karcevskij had brought Saussure's ideas from Geneva to Moscow (Jakobson, 1956c:SW II 518). In 1917, a Russian student of Husserl's, Gustav Špet, drew Jakobson's attention to Marty's descriptive philosophy of language. Marty (1908) also propounded the idea of a universal grammar, although, in contrast to Husserl, with a more empirical and psychological orientation (Jakobson, 1974e:12f., 21f.).

Jakobson frequently elucidates Saussure's ideas in the light of his historical predecessors. He traces the fundamental semiotic distinction between *signifiant* and *signifié* and the relational determination of the *signifiants* back to the Stoic innovators of semiotics in antiquity, to the scholastics of the Middle Ages, and even to the treatises of ancient Indian grammarians (1960a:SW II 394ff.; 1965b:SW II 345; 1975b). For the concept of system and for opposition as a fundamental relation, he refers (1933:SW II 543; 1974e:12ff.) to Hegel and thus endows Saussure's static dualism with a dynamic and dialectic unity.

Depending on the context, Saussure serves the Prague linguists as a model to be propagated, as a companion in arms in the avant-garde, and as a rival against whom to measure their own conceptions. Jakobson (1921a:18) was probably one of the first to cite Saussure's *Cours* in a non-French publication. At the First International Congress of Linguists in The Hague, three members of the Prague Circle, Jakobson, Mathesius, and Trubetzkoy, joined forces with Bally and Sechehaye from Geneva to draft common theses (1928c: 85f.). Saussure's *Cours* became the underlying, permanent model, the background against which the Prague linguists made further discoveries. At a meeting of the *Cercle linguistique de Prague* on January 13, 1927 (1928a:SW I 1f.), Jakobson for the first time publicly argued the thesis which he subsequently propounded at the congress at The Hague (1928b:4ff.), namely, that diachrony, contrary to Saussure's view, must be classed as an integral component in the linguistic system. The following pages attempt a systematic delineation of the relationship between synchrony and diachrony and of Jakobson's additions, deletions, and refinements to that relationship, especially with respect to the concepts of the phoneme and opposition, the dichotomy *langue/parole*, the two axes of language, and the two principles of the arbitrariness and linearity of linguistic signs.

In reference to Saussure, Jakobson (1939a:SW I 294) distinguishes two categories of scientific masterworks: those which outline the tendencies and achievements of a school and present a rounded, thoroughly elaborated system of thought, and those which mark the promising beginnings of a trend rather than its ultimate success and thus offer the prelude to novel, bold exploration instead of a self-contained final doctrine. Saussure's *Cours* belongs to the latter category.

> The volume stands on the dividing line between two epochs and two approaches; a book of this kind, no matter how ingenious, can never be completely devoid of contradiction. It would be dangerous and inappropriate—although it is unfortunately often so done—to view the *Cours de linguistique* as a compendium, as a cut and polished doctrine, and either to gloss over its contradictions or to lose sight of its fundamentals because of them.

R. Engler's critical edition of the original notes (Saussure, 1967ff.) for this trailblazing work confirms Jakobson's 1939 evaluation. Much of what Saussure proposed merely as a possibility, as a question, or in otherwise subtilized and differentiated form, appears as simple and definitive doctrine in the edition compiled by his students (see Jakobson, 1975f).

1.4.5. *Mathematics.* The concept of structure became a focal point in mathematics through the development of the calculus of variations in the 1870s and of topology at the turn of the century. The final breakthrough came in the late thirties with the Bourbaki group's elaboration of matrices, through whose differentiation and combination one can derive the structures of the various branches of mathematics. Structure is defined as the set of relations which links up the elements of a system. An extensional version of the mathematical definition of structure found its way into analytical philosophy via Russell (1919:59ff.) and Carnap (1928:21ff.), who understood a description of structure to be an investigation of the formal properties of a relation, which can be formulated without reference to the meaning of the relation or the type of objects between which the relation occurs. The structure of a relation P is thus defined as the class of relations isomorphic to P.

Jakobson is above all attracted by the concept of invariance in the mathematical theories of structure, with their target of extracting the relational invariants of a set of elements. In his historical commentaries on modern linguistics, Jakobson usually cites first Klein's *Erlanger Programm* (1872:463f.).

> Thus as a generalization of geometry, the following comprehensive problem arises. A multiplicity is given and in it a transformational group; the constituents of the multiplicity should be investigated with regard to those properties which are not affected by the transformations of the given group. In conformance with modern terminology, . . . one could also say: . . . One must develop the theory of invariants belonging to the group. (1972a:73)

Herewith Jakobson draws upon the same mathematical trend as Husserl, who as a student of mathematics wrote a dissertation on the calculus of variations (1882), which may well have inspired his famous method of free variation for the retrieval of invariant, essential properties, and relations.

Two types of variation may be distinguished. In the first type, single (concrete and abstract) properties of a set of elements change while others remain invariant. Thus, to cite Klein's example, the properties of a spatial entity remain unchanged through all movements of space, through its transformations of similarity, and through the process of mirroring. Husserl and Jakobson (see 1956a:SW I 483) treat this type of variation in particular. The essential is divorced from the inessential. In the second type, the material elements as such are exchanged. Numbers, for instance, are replaced by figures or arrangements of letters. Here only the abstract structure remains invariant, though undergoing different concrete representations. This type of variation, which separates the abstract from the concrete, receives special consideration from Lévi-Strauss. Lévi-Strauss tries, for example, to demonstrate that nourishment, the culinary triangle of raw, cooked, and rotten foods, reveals the same structure as one of the first and most universal stages in the build-up of the phonological system.

Jakobson further emphasizes the convergence between mathematics and linguistics in focusing on relational properties. For topology, Jakobson (1962a:SW I 637) cites the historian of mathematics, E. T. Bell: "It is not the things that matter but the relations between them." Jakobson also points out that the same year, 1916, witnessed the publication of Einstein's general theory of relativity and Saussure's *Cours*, in which the ultimate entities of language are presented as relative data. On the other hand, we will show in the section on synchrony and diachrony how the dynamic and flexible conception of time and simultaneity developed for physics by Einstein inspired Jakobson to surmount the rigid dichotomy of synchrony and diachrony propounded by Saussure.

1.4.6. *Art.* When asked what inspired the new conception of language and linguistics in the Moscow and Prague Circles, Jakobson regularly cites as most important the avant-garde trends in painting, poetry, and music immediately preceding the First World War. The scientific sources of Jakobson's structuralism mentioned so far are all of secondary significance. They merely provide the first scientific formulations and early concrete adaptations of intuitions which had been attained in art and through contact with artists.

What fascinated the literary scholars of Moscow and Prague in the work of these artists were the very same themes which we have already encountered in the scientific movements, i.e., the inquiry into the relations among different tenses, which appear extremely dynamic, flexible, and even reversible in the new art trends (Jakobson, from 1919:27f. to 1972a:80), and also the stress on invariance in multiplicity and the relations between wholes and parts. Bracque's credo, "I do not believe in things, I believe only in their relationship" (cited by Jakobson, 1962a:SW I 632), coincides almost literally with Bell's statement cited above. Finally, we have the semiotic orientation of these schools of art, especially cubism with its experimental destruction and explorative transformation of the relations connecting *signans, signatum,* and *denotatum.*

The mode in which the *signatum* stands relatively to the *signans,* on the one hand, and to the *denotatum,* on the other, had never been laid bare so plainly, nor the semantic problems of art brought forward so provocatively as in cubist pictures, which delay recognition of the transformed and obscured object or even reduce it to zero. In order to enliven the inward and outward relationships of the visual signs, one had, as Picasso said, "to break, to make one's revolution and start at zero." (1962a:SW I 632)

The experimental and methodologically reflected approach developed in painting by cubism was taken over by the Russian futurists and applied to poetry. "The word as such" (*Slovo kak takovoe*), as the first manifesto of the futuristic poets was entitled, and the relations inherent to it were investigated theoretically and also poetically in the literal sense of the word, i.e., practically. Among the futuristic poets, Vladimir Majakovskij not only took an active part in the discussions of the Moscow Linguistic Circle, he also found inspiration in the theoretical analyses and reports of the young field workers in folklore. Jakobson (1971a:41) describes how the sequence *bar — ban' — baraban* in Majakovskij's poem "150 000 000" always reminds him of his report on a paronomastic pun in a folklore tale about a landowner (*barin*) who was beaten up with "drumbeats" (*otbarabanil*) by a farmer in a bathhouse (*banja*).

In the work of these artists, we come upon the source of another feature of structuralism already alluded to in connection with the "antipsychologism" of Husserlian phenomenology, the recognition of the autonomy of the domain of every object. The involvement with poetry was ideal for the discovery of such a methodological principle. Poetry differs from other forms of linguistic application in that the linguistic medium becomes the keynote of perception and an autonomous focus of interest. In poetry the specifically linguistic devices, relegated to the background in prose for the sake of the content of the discourse, become palpable or perceivable, as the Russian formalists would say.

2.
Philosophical
and Methodological
Principles

With current critiques of structuralism as a point of departure, we shall concretize the character of Jakobson's understanding of structural linguistics and the science of literature. Confronted with Jakobson's version of structuralism, these critiques can almost all be shelved as shortsighted. Not only do they miss the mark, the problems posed have for the most part been treated by Jakobson himself with more sophistication. We cite them only as a contrasting background against which the *philosophie latente* underlying Jakobson's work can be highlighted.

2.1. *Synchrony and diachrony*

2.1.1. *Saussure's antithesis and Jakobson's synthesis.* In a trailblazing repudiation of the one-sided historical approach of nineteenth century linguistics, Saussure advanced the dichotomy of synchronic and diachronic linguistics and the primacy of synchronic description as a methodological principle.

Certainly all sciences would profit by indicating more precisely the coordinates along which their subject matter is aligned. Everywhere, distinctions should be made, according to the following illustration [see Figure 2], between (1) the axis of simultaneities (AB), which stands for the relations of coexisting things and from which the intervention of time is excluded; and (2) the axis of successions (CD), on which only one thing can be considered at a time but upon which are located all the things on the first axis together with their changes. (1916: 79f.)

In the discussion on structuralism, argumentation is not infrequently based on the assumption that Saussure and his followers ignored the historical dimension altogether and reduced the field of investigation in the sciences to a static system. There then ensues a zealous defense of the truism that there is not only a synchronic system but also a diachronic history. Saussure's defenders (De Mauro, 1972:453) reply by pointing out the purely methodological character of the dichotomy: Saussure simply sets up an antithesis of viewpoints.

However, it is this methodological character that Jakobson finds problematic. In clarifying it, we distinguish two questions. (1) Is the methodological opposition of synchronic and diachronic linguistics based only on the two-fold temporal form in which linguistic phenomena occur, the form of simultaneity and the form of succession? (2) Is there not after all an inner affinity between structuralism and static synchronism? To quote a critic (Reiter, 1970:174), do not the real occurrences themselves threaten to be swallowed by a timeless *identity* as a result of the exclusive concentration on *invariants* and *constants*; or, as Sartre (1966:95) fears, might not the concentration on structures cause one to lose sight of the possibility of surmounting them?

Regarding the first question, Jakobson criticizes Saussure's methodological distinction as being guided by an untenable identification of the opposing pair, synchrony/diachrony, with the actually conclusive opposing pairs, systematic (structural)/casual (atomistic), teleological/mechanistic, and static/dynamic.

Synchrony	*Diachrony*
systematic	casual
teleological	mechanistic
static	dynamic

The assignment of the first two opposing pairs results in a formal disqualification of diachrony, while the third devaluates synchrony, to which Saussure gives priority. From the countless passages in which Jakobson since 1919 (27f.) has commented on the relationship between the present and history, we select a few key passages.

Saussure's teaching that sound changes are destructive factors, fortuitous and blind, limits the active role of the speech community to sensing each given stage of deviations from the customary linguistic pattern as an orderly system. This antinomy between synchronic and diachronic linguistic studies should be overcome by a transformation of historical phonetics into the history of the phonemic system. In other words, phonetic changes must be analyzed in relation to the phonemic system which undergoes these mutations. For instance, if the order within a linguistic system is disturbed, there follows a cycle of sound changes aimed at its renewed stabilization (like in a game of chess). (1928a:SW I 2)

The question of the goal of a phonetic event is gaining ascendance for the linguist over the traditional question of causes. One transcends the tradition of the "neogrammarians," not by renouncing the concept of "phonetic law," but rather by interpreting this concept teleologically and abandoning the mechanistic concept. To the extent that phonetic changes are treated without consideration of the phonological system that undergoes them, the laws of general phonetics remain in the dark. (1928b:SW I 6)

It seems to me that the great mistake and confusion, the sharp separation between synchrony and diachrony, was to a high degree due to a confusion between two dichotomies. One is the dichotomy of synchrony and diachrony, and the other is the

dichotomy between static and dynamic. Synchronic is not equal
to static. When at a movie I ask you what you see at a given
moment on the screen, you won't see statics—you'll see horses
running, people walking, and other movements. Where do you see
statics? Only on the billboards. The billboard is static but not
necessarily synchronic. Suppose a billboard remains unchanged
for a year—that is static. And it is completely legitimate to ask
what is static in linguistic diachrony . . . what has been static,
unchangeable, immutable in Slavic from the early Middle Ages
. . . until the present. This is a static problem but at the same time
a diachronic one. (1953b:SW II 562)

The liaison between statics and dynamics is one of the most
fundamental dialectic antinomies that determine the concept of
language. The dialectic of linguistic development cannot be
grasped without reference to this antinomy. The attempts to
identify *synchrony, diachrony,* and the domain of application of
teleology on the one hand, and *diachrony, dynamics,* and the
sphere of *mechanic causality* on the other illegitimately narrow
the framework of synchrony, reduce historical linguistics to an
accumulation of isolated facts, and create the harmful illusion of
an abyss between the problems of synchrony and diachrony.
(1931a:SW I 220)

In Saussure, the synchronic and diachronic axes are anti-
(or hetero-) nomically juxtaposed. In Jakobson, they form an
homonomous unity. Both contain static and dynamic aspects. Both find themselves oriented toward the same system
in a teleological arrangement.

2.1.2. *The heightening of synchrony.* Saussure's fundamental idea is that linguistic elements cannot be viewed in
isolation since their value consistently proves to be a function
of the other elements. Language is a system, i.e., a whole,
whose parts are interdependent or, as Saussure expresses it,
whose units are bound by solidarities.

For Saussure's (1916:115f.) argumentation we select an
illustration from Jakobson (1959a:SW II 261). The English
word *cheese* can have the same meaning as the Russian *syr.* It
does not, however, have the same value, since cottage cheese
is a kind of cheese but is not *syr.* The Russians say, *prinesi
syru i tvorogu,* ("bring cheese and cottage cheese"). The

difference in value between *cheese* and *syr* stems from the fact that *syr* is accompanied by a second term, while *cheese* is not.

In this illustration, the value of the linguistic sign is not defined positively by its content, but negatively by its contrastive position to the remaining signs of the system. However, the value of the sign can also be positively determined by a relation of similarity and additionally enriched. Thus, *dix-neuf* owes its value not only to its contrastive position to other numerals, *un, deux, vingt,* etc., but also to its relation of similarity with numerals such as *dix-sept, dix-huit, vingt-neuf, trente-neuf,* etc., with which it forms a common series (Saussure, 1916:131). An illustration of a revaluation internal to the system is the French word *décrépit.*

> Latin *crispus* 'crisp' provided French with the root *crép-* from which were formed the verbs *crépir* 'rough-cast' and *décrépir* 'remove mortar'. Against this, at a certain moment the word *decrepitus,* of unknown origin, was borrowed from Latin and became *décrépit* 'decrepit'. Certainly today the community of speakers sets up a relation between *un mur décrépi* 'a wall from which mortar is falling' and *un homme décrépit* 'a decrepit man', although historically the two words have nothing in common; people often speak of the *façade décrépite* of a house. And this is static, for it concerns the relation between two coexisting forms of language. (Saussure, 1916:83)

The relations of similarity and opposition have a teleological character. Their function is to enable sense-identification and sense-differentiation.

In Saussure, the system-bound determination of value is restricted to an unextended and static line of simultaneity. Jakobson breaks through this restriction. The value of linguistic data is not determined by factually coexistent data alone, but equally by temporally antecedent and anticipatory data. It is not an objective simultaneity, but the subjective experience of simultaneity that counts. Past, present, and future occurrences can coexist in the subjective experience of time.

The facts experienced as existing simultaneously as such by a community of speaking subjects are not the object of synchronic linguistics, but rather the facts experienced simultaneously, i.e., constituting the content of the linguistic conscious at a given moment. In the conscious of the speaking subject, some facts can be closely associated with the present, while others . . . can refer to the past or gravitate toward the future. (1929a:SW I 20)

Jakobson's favorite example stems from his own experience.

There has occurred a certain salient change in the vowel pattern of contemporary Standard Russian. In the unstressed, especially pretonic position, the two phonemes /e/ and /i/ were distinguished by our grandparents' generation in Moscow. In the parlance of our and the younger generation, these two phonemes merged in one /i/. For the intermediate generation, that of our parents, this distinction is optional. . . . When the time factor enters into such a system of symbolic values as language, it becomes a symbol itself and may be used as a stylistic means. For instance, when we speak in a more conservative way, we use the more archaic forms. In Moscow Russian, the generation of our parents did not use the distinction between unstressed /e/ and /i/ in familiar talk: rather the newer fashion of fusing both phonemes was followed to produce the impression of being younger than one really was. (1953b:SW II 562f.)

Not only on the level of phonology, but also on the levels of syntax and semantics, and not only in everyday language, but in poetry as well, linguistic forms typical of an epoch extend into subsequent times, surviving in them as archaisms. In every period, modernisms are also active, trying to install themselves as forms of expression of the future, and thus *ipso facto* determining the value of the current forms. The time factor becomes for Jakobson a highly dynamic value factor (1923:27f.).

Saussure's dichotomy relies on the rigid conception of time in classical physics. The present dwindles to an unextended thread. Jakobson's time conception, on the other hand, is inspired by cubist and futurist art and literature. He seeks to adapt their dynamic experience of time, which overflows the present moment, to linguistic findings, with the support also of concepts from Einstein's theory of relativity and from the up-and-coming phenomenological analyses of the consciousness of time.

> The new doctrine denies the absolute nature of time and, concomitantly, the existence of a universal time. Each system in movement possesses its own time, the speed of the flow of time is not the same. (1919:28)†

Saussure's scheme of time takes the form of cross hairs, while that of the Prague structuralists is a prism in which the horizontal axis of the objective time sequence is projected onto the vertical axis of subjective simultaneity. What counts is not objective time but rather subjectively experienced time.

Saussure's cross hairs *   The Prague prism **

```
a ── b ── c ── d ── e
     |    |    |    |
     a    b    c    d
          |    |    |
          a    b    c
               |    |
               a    b
                    |
                    a
```

*We adopt Jakobson's version (1939a:SW I 306) of Saussure's scheme (1916:80), to facilitate comparison with the Prague prism. Jakobson takes the vertical line for the axis of simultaneity and the horizontal line for the axis of succession, allowing better coordination with the paradigmatic and syntagmatic axes (see section 3.1.).

**This scheme, slightly adapted, has been taken from J. Mukařovský (1940:117). P. and W. Steiner (1976:81ff.) suggest that Mukařovský's scheme may have been inspired by Husserl's analyses of time-consciousness (1928/1966:28 [389]; see 199, 330f.). Jakobson (1923:42ff.) himself, in discussing how time is experienced in poetry, makes reference to V. Benussi (1913), a student of A. Meinong who had studied with Brentano and corresponded with Husserl for many years.

Figure 2

†Quotation from the manifesto of futurist painters. See also 1972a:80.

2.1.3. *The equality of diachrony.* Saussure recognized a functionally guided system only on the axis of simultaneity. For the axis of succession, he adopted the dogma of the neogrammarians, according to whom the events of the history of language are to be explained on mechanistic-causal grounds, on the basis of causes occurring by chance and atomistically. These causes, mostly of a physiological and psychological nature, are not only foreign to the system of linguistic values, they have a destructive effect on it.

One need not delve far into the literature of the neogrammarians to encounter the bias which blinded them to the teleological, system-relatedness of language change. As with modern philosophy's critique of the metaphysical principle of teleology, the positivistic movement of the late nineteenth century accepted a functional explanation only for conscious actions or in the form of the principle of least effort. Sound change, however, the main concern of the neogrammarians, is—at least according to their findings—a largely unconscious process. Thus all that remained of the teleological explanation was the economic principle of least effort. It was too obvious that this principle could be enlisted for only some of the changes. For an excessive proportion, the criteria for the degree of effort were either highly disputable or, on the contrary, the increased effort was perfectly indisputable. This resulted in an unsystematic, atomistic explanation sometimes based on the above principle (cf. also Saussure, 1916:204f.), sometimes based on an antecedent change of the speech organs which was in turn thought to be mechanistically caused, sometimes based on climatic influences, and so on (Osthoff, 1879). To support the principle that the physiological laws of sound change admit of no exception,* recourse was taken to a psychological explanation, to the law of analogy. The association of similarity and the imitative instinct not only have to answer

*One of the promotors of the principle of no exception in sound laws is the same J. Winteler (1876; see Osthoff and Brugmann, 1878:202) whom Trubetzkoy (1933:227; see Jakobson, 1972a:75) wrested from obscurity as the inventor of the dual—phonological and phonetic—analysis of sound.

for the finding that a sound shift arising out of a physiological change in the speech organs of individual persons
becomes a general phenomenon, but for the explanation of
irregularities as well. Deviations, according to the neogrammarians, occur through the adaptation of certain linguistic
forms to others which are similar to them.

In a memorable session of the *Cercle linguistique de
Prague* on January 13, 1927, three months after it was
founded, the thirty-year-old Jakobson took the floor and
claimed to have found not only the universal principle of
sound change, but also at long last a satisfactory argument
for the principle of sound laws admitting of no exception
(1928a:SW I 1f.). A later reviewer (Ivić, 1965:38, 42) calls
this discovery "a milestone in the history of phonology" and
the consequent painstaking monograph on the phonological
evolution of Russian "the greatest event in the development
of diachronic methods since the Neo-grammarian breakthrough in the 1870's." In a somewhat later declaration of
principles, Jakobson's discovery reads:

> Phonology countered the isolationistic method of the neogram-
> marians with an *integral method*; each phonological entity is
> treated as a partial whole which unfolds in relation to other
> partial wholes of different higher orders. The first principle of
> historical phonology thus reads: *Every change is to be treated as a
> function of the system within which it occurs.* A sound change
> can only be comprehended by elucidating its role in the system of
> the language. (1931a:SW I 202f.)

Jakobson does not—as do the neogrammarians—proceed
from the history of language to the study of sound laws, but
rather from the "two most intentional structures of language" (1939b:SW I 313), poetic and literary language. He is,
therefore, no stranger to the functional coordination of all
the individual parts aiming at a closed whole. Correspondingly, he does not interpret the teleological principle metaphysically as in Aristotelian philosophy, or economically as
in the natural sciences of the nineteenth century, but rather
purely logically and phenomenologically. The teleological

principle makes it possible to order a number of phenomena according to their immanent and systematic aspects (2.4.3. below).

The most obvious form of system-oriented sound change is the restoration of balance within a system. If the first sound *p* in a series *p, t, k* has changed into a *b*, the outcome is an asymmetric series *b, t, k*. The simplest way to restore the former symmetry of three identically tuned stops without making the process retrogressive is an analogous modification of the other unvoiced stops. The equivalence of structure is then reestablished in the new series *b, d, g.* Should such a series already exist, then the older, more comprehensive system can survive only if the former series *b, d, g* itself undergoes a mutation, e.g., aspiration.

This illustration, chosen for its simplicity and widespread familiarity, does not stem from Jakobson but from Sapir (1921:182), who had independently discovered the dependence of sound changes on the system before Jakobson. Saussure, too (1916:125f.), had already hinted at this dependence with the example of the chess game. But it was Jakobson who transcended the domain of flashes of inspiration and isolated illustration. He was the first to work this inspiration into a systematic theory (1931a) and to apply it to an entire aspect of language in a detailed monograph (1929a), thus rendering it for the first time historically effective. He was also the first to propose a system-immanent explanation for the transient upset of an established balance. Restorative tendencies cannot go into action unless preceded by the disruption of an existing harmony.

The offensive role of the system is not quite as easy to verify as the defensive role. Decisive here is a fundamental condition for the functioning of language, namely the availability of an ample stock of differentiated signs. The same applies equally, if not more, to the designation of objects for the stylistic expression of emotions. Jakobson (1931a:SW I 219) sees the first step toward a modification of the phonological system as being taken above all through the active exploitation of the phonetic, *in se* meaningless variants

of a sound system and through the intentional or uninten-
tional neglect of phonological, meaning-differentiating variations in affective discourse and in poetic language. The
adoption of foreign words can be cited as an illustration here
inasmuch as the borrowing language, instead of molding
pronunciation to its own system, has retained foreign
pronunciation as a stylistic device, e.g., to identify the
speaker as foreign and different or as cultivated and
cosmopolitan. A language accepts foreign elements, however,
only insofar as they correspond to its own developmental
tendencies. Foreign language influence can be viewed neither
as necessary nor as sufficient grounds for modification, but
rather only as a welcome circumstance, which is exploited for
the inner needs of the system. The needs of the system
determine the choice and direction of "contamination" by
another language (1938:SW I 239, 241).

> Russian and other Slavic languages as well have borrowed a great
> many foreign words with the phoneme *f.* In those cases which
> tended thoroughly to russify the loan word with *f,* the *f* was
> replaced by *xv, x,* or *p. F* indicated the foreignness of a word, and
> people sometimes inserted it in loan words where it did not in
> fact belong, e.g., *kufárka* instead of *kuxárka* (a cook), etc.
> Gradually, however, some of the words that had retained the *f*
> (*fonar', lif, fílin, Fédja,* etc.) were assimilated with Russian
> indigenous words, and the fundamental Russian archiphoneme

$\boxed{v, v'}$ became enriched by two new phonemes:

$\boxed{\begin{array}{c} v, v' \\ f, f' \end{array}}$. (1931a:SW I 209)

Nevertheless, there still remains a certain indetermination in the development of language as regards the
direction and speed of development. A choice of possibilities
is available at every stage. The time of mutation varies from
system to system. The development is limited only by the
laws of foundedness, to which the sound system owes its

hierarchically structured unity, and by certain less strict and only statistically ascertainable trends which mark individual languages.

The laws of foundedness (*a* founds *b,* etc.) can be reformulated in terms of laws of implication. They express the compatibility and incompatibility of linguistic data (see 1929a:SW I 22).

1. If *a* exists, then *b* exists too.
2. If *a* exists, then *b, c,* and *d* are possible.*
3. If *a* exists, then *b* is absent.
4. If *a* is absent, then *b* is absent too.

These laws are universal and panchronic. They are to be found in all sound systems and act both as laws of the static balance of languages and as determinants in their build-up (in the child's acquisition of language and, as follows logically, in the initial genesis of the languages of the world), in their modification (in the development of languages), and in their break-down (in aphasic disorders).

> A differentiation of rounded vowels according to degree of aperture cannot arise in child language as long as the same opposition is lacking for the unrounded vowels. The pair $u \sim o$ cannot, therefore, precede the pair $i \sim e,$ and there are no children who have an *o*-phoneme without having acquired an *e*-phoneme. On the contrary *o* is very often acquired considerably later than *e.* Accordingly, a number of languages have an *e*-phoneme without any *o*-phoneme . . . , but there is hardly any language with *o* and not *e.* (1941:SW I 365)

Indetermination rests on the versatile compatibility of certain linguistic phenomena. But even in such basically open cases, some lines of development possess greater probability than others. Languages have their developmental tendencies. English, for instance, is conspicuous for its tendency to lose

---

*Formulation of the law of compatibility in analogy to Jakobson's formulation of the other laws has been undertaken by the author.

morphological elements. Jakobson cites an analogous observation made by L. Tisza in quantum mechanics.

> "Quantum mechanics is morphically deterministic, whereas the
> temporal processes, the transitions between stationary states, are
> governed by statistical laws." In other words, structural linguistics
> as well as "quantum mechanics gains in morphic determinism
> what it loses in temporal determinism." (1953a:SW II 227)

Yet, does not the axis of diachrony through this
indetermination undergo a formal devaluation in contrast to
the axis of synchrony? Not at all. The indetermination of
evolution can be compared to the vagueness of most concepts
from a static point of view. There is no exact criterion for
calling a geographical place a city or a town. A place becomes
a city legally only when its population exceeds 10,000.
Sociologically, it may already long have been urban in
character. Strict determination of one criterion entails greater
arbitrariness for another. The criterion of population count
can only be fixed at the cost of the criterion of a
"comprehensive" availability of goods. But these two criteria
are vague as well. Who has more right to be called a
resident—the person who works and lives in the city during
the week and goes home to the country on weekends or the
person who does the opposite? And how comprehensive is
the colloquial "everything" that one can buy in the city?
Yet, even here, what appears to be "fluid" cannot simply be
equated with "arbitrary." It remains "restricted to a set of
structural types" (Husserl, 1931:51). In spite of the fluid
boundaries of the referents, no one considers the terms *city*
and *town* synonymous and interchangeable.

2.1.4. *The historical and dynamic bias of the most important
structural laws.* The second question raised at the beginning
of this chapter concerns the problem of the affinity between
structuralism and static synchronism. A critique which tends
to assume such an affinity overlooks two things which have
been elaborated in Jakobson's work—the pronounced, historical bias of both primary structures, and the open, variable
form of synchrony, i.e., of the historical situation.

The two major structures in Jakobson's linguistic system are hierarchical stratification and opposition. Hierarchical stratification is based on the laws of foundedness enumerated above. A relation of foundedness, according to Husserl's formulation (1913:466f.) which Jakobson (1941:SW I 360) adopted, can be "(a) reciprocal, (b) one-sided, according as the law in question is convertible or not."

reciprocal foundedness: if *a*, then *b*, and if *b*, then *a*.

one-sided foundedness: if *a*, then *b*, but not if *b*, then *a*.

The laws of one-sided foundedness, actually abstract logical laws, positively invite an historical interpretation when applied to concrete phenomena:

If *a* occurs, then *b* must have occurred "before."

If *a* disappears, then *b* must have disappeared "before."

Faced with the laws of one-sided foundedness, the question no longer reads, is structuralism open to history, but rather, does it do justice to history; does it not, with its hierarchical stratification, abet a long buried belief in progress? A distinction, however, must be made here between the build-up of a linguistic system in the individual child's acquisition of language and in the genesis of the first languages of man and the continuous modification of the system in the evolution of different languages and dialects. One-sided progress is naturally to be found in the first stages of the child's acquisition of language and can also be logically assumed for the earliest stages of the genesis of man's first languages. On the other hand, the changes in languages whose history is known to us present no picture of a progressive build-up, but rather the picture of constant modification, whereby build-up and break-down offset each other (see 1931a:SW I 215ff.). Modern languages do not differ from ancient languages through higher level phonological or grammatical systems, but at most through more extensive vocabulary and highly specialized phraseology in abstract and technical spheres. Brøndal's "law of compensation" (Brøndal, 1940:107; Jakobson, 1944:SW II 487) comes into play in the interrelation of the various languages. Languages with a prominent and complex development in regard to one category stand at a relatively simple and low level in regard to other categories.

From the point of view of structuralism, opposition is the basic driving principle, both methodologically and objectively. An exclusive orientation toward the invariant would, therefore, have to be rejected as poor structuralism. Good structuralism keeps both invariance and variation in mind and stresses their dialectic. What in one system appears as a phonetic variation of one and the same phoneme can, in another system, occur as the invariant phonological feature of a series of variants. Thus, in English, the light and dark *l* are two variants of one and the same phoneme, while in Polish they act as two oppositional phonemes. Furthermore, findings in two coexistent systems may also be encountered in successive stages of one and the same system. Two phonetic variants of one phoneme can become two phonological invariants (e.g., *k* and *c* in Latvian; 1931a:SW I 208), and two phonological invariants can become phonetic variants of one single phoneme (e.g., ʒ and *z* in Japanese; ibid., 206).

We have already touched upon the formation of opposition in phonology as a modifying factor of the system. Jakobson writes of its historic effect mainly in terms of poetry. Poetry, with its intention of making the linguistic medium as such conscious, impels language to overcome the automatism and imperceptibility of structures by heightening and systematically utilizing differences that arise, which—to repeat—goes as far as "shifts in the phonological structure" (1931a:SW I 219). In order to make us aware of a hidden process of language, the poet uses it in place of a familiar procedure of the existing poetic tradition or of ordinary, everyday language. "Only on the background of the familiar does the unfamiliar reach and surprise us" (1921a:63). The emancipation of the sign from its reference to the object, as it is practiced by futuristic poetry, is a reaction to the object-fetishism of naturalism. Similarly, Pasternak's metonymic style is to be understood in contrast to the metaphorical structure of Majakovskij's poetry (1935a: 140ff.).

With Baudouin de Courtenay (see Jakobson, 1960a:SW II 421) and Saussure (1916:205), Jakobson insists on the unceasing competition between centrifugal and centripetal forces in language. The tendency toward divergence and variation, nourished by a particularistic attitude and desig- nated as *parochialism* by Saussure and Jakobson due to its extreme form, leads to the emergence of territorial and social dialects and also to individualistic creations in literature. The tendency toward convergence and invariance is nourished by the objective of intersubjective communication, which demands a uniform or generalized code.

2.1.5. *The open form of situation.* We have already juxtaposed Jakobson's more detailed concept of synchrony with Saussure's narrow concept. We next confront it with the concept of situation in existential philosophy. The most vehement attack on the alleged antagonism of structuralism to history issued from existential philosophy. In Saussure and Jakobson's conception of diachrony, destructive chance and determination by the system were shown to be opposed; in the confrontation with existential philosophy, creative freedom replaces destructive chance as the counterpart of dependence upon the system. Our investigation will show that Jakobson's concept of situation endows historical change and the historical understanding of such change with a more adequate foundation than that supplied by the egocentric concept of situation in existential philosophy.

Existential philosophy views freedom and situation as correlative concepts. "There is freedom only in a situation, and there is a situation only through freedom" (Sartre, 1943:489). Analyzing primary sources and observing the direction taken by the historical and literary sciences under the influence of existential philosophy, one is led to conclude that situation remains the dominant partner. Freedom in its principal function just suffices for me to realize my historical situation as such and not to be deposited like a stone in the riverbed of time. A look at the peak of the mountain, through which I transcend my location, enables me to situate myself at just this location, still far away from the peak. Freedom is limited by my situation at the time. I can manage to see another situation only from the perspective of my point of view. In keeping with this conception, I experience a look at me by someone else from another location as alienation (Sartre, 1943:525ff.).

The direction taken by hermeneutics under the guidance of existential philosophy is revealing. The target of Schleiermacher's hermeneutics was the historically faithful reproduction of an old text. The proponents of hermeneutics in existential philosophy were ultimately concerned with their own understanding of themselves through study of the old texts, with the confirmation and shaping of the prejudices idealized to a transcendental necessity, which govern their Weltanschauung. Thus it is illusion and misguided endeavor to seek, for example, an historical reconstruction of Joan of Arc's motives. With narcissistic pleasure, the observation is made that one's own situation is reflected again and again in an historical or mythological figure. According to my respective situation, Joan appears to me as a mystic the day before yesterday, as a champion of liberalism yesterday, as a social revolutionary today, and as a child of nature tomorrow. The aim is not to rise above one's situation, but to become ensconced in it. "What is decisive is not to get out of the circle but to come into it in the right way" (Heidegger, 1927:195).

The concept of situation in existential philosophy, as in Saussure, is imprisoned in the classical, perspectivistic theory of perception. According to Saussure (1916:81f.), "it would be absurd to attempt to sketch a panorama of the Alps by viewing them simultaneously from several peaks of the Jura; a panorama must be made from a single vantage point." Jakobson approaches perception from a completely different angle, namely from cubism.

> In the nineteenth century . . . the artist is the slave of routine, he
> consciously ignores ordinary and scientific experience. . . . As if
> we knew the object from only one vantage point, from only one
> facet, as if having seen the face we forget the existence of the
> nape of the neck, as if the nape were the other side of the moon,
> unknown and invisible. Just like the old novels, in which we are
> informed of events only to the extent that the hero himself is
> aware of them. Painting did once attempt to double the view of
> the object, justified by the reflection of the landscape or object in
> water or in a mirror. . . . However, it was cubism that canonized
> the plurality of points of view. (1919:25)

An historical situation for Jakobson never coincides
with a single, ultimate, mono-perspective point of view, upon
which one only falls back with every attempt to break loose.
The subject finds himself in an open theater where he can
occupy different seats. In each phase of history there are at
least two possibilities, namely, to act like a conservative or a
progressive (1953b:SW II 562; 1956a:SW I 502).

> Any verbal code is convertible and necessarily comprises a set of
> distinct subcodes or, in other words, functional varieties of
> language. Any speech community has at its disposal a) more
> explicit and more elliptic patterns, with an orderly scale of
> transitions from a maximal explicitness to an extreme ellipsis, b)
> a purposive alternation of more archaic and newfangled dictions,
> c) a patent difference between rules of ceremonial, formal, and
> informal, slovenly speech. (1974e:37)

Language is not monolithic. The code at the disposal of man
for intersubjective communication is a convertible code, a
transformational system by means of which a message can be
translated from subcode to subcode, from sign system to sign
system.

Code switching is an inherent possibility of conversation. Without translatability, intersubjective communication would not be possible. Bilingualism is not an exception but only a particularly plain example of a general
finding and can thus serve as a model.

Everyone, when speaking to a new person, tries, deliberately or involuntarily, to hit upon a common vocabulary: either to please or simply to be understood or, finally to bring him out, he uses the terms of his addressee. (1953b:SW II 559)

Without intralingual transformation, i.e., without changing the point of view, a child would not be able to learn his language at all. Just as an adult learns neologisms and new expressions through translation into his familiar vocabulary and through paraphrasing, a child acquires his lexicon and his grammar through demarcation on the basis of the speech he has so far mastered. In fact, he loves to make his progress clear to himself by repeatedly playing on words.

A typical property of children's speech is an intimate interlacement of two functions—the metalingual and the poetic one—which in adult language are quite separate. Although the pivotal role which in language learning belongs to the acquisition of metalanguage is well-known, the predominantly metalingual concern of the somnolent child with language itself comes as a great surprise. It shows us the ways in which language is gradually mastered. Many of the recorded passages bear a striking resemblance to the grammatical and lexical exercises in textbooks for self-instruction in foreign languages: "What color—What color blanket—What color mop—What color glass. . . . Not the yellow blanket—The white. . . . It's not black—It's yellow . . . Not yellow—Red. . . . (1962c:SW II 286)

A child learns a language not only by learning the rules that tell him in which extralinguistic situation he can use which linguistic elements. He also learns which basic forms can be transferred to which higher-level and more complex forms. He learns to reword an utterance. He has to know which linguistic elements he can or cannot use in a given context. The contextual application yields information about the value, the limits of meaning, of a sign.

Suppose I want to explain to a unilingual Indian what Chesterfield is, and I point to a package of cigarettes. What can the

Indian conclude? He doesn't know whether I mean this package
in particular, or a package in general, one cigarette or many, a
certain brand or cigarettes in general, or, still more generally,
something to smoke, or, universally, any agreeable thing. He
doesn't know, moreover, whether I'm simply showing, giving,
selling, or prohibiting the cigarettes to him. He will gather what
Chesterfield is, and what it is not, only if he masters a series of
other linguistic signs which will serve as interpretant of the sign
under discussion. (1953b:SW II 566f.)

The real revolution in language acquisition occurs when
the child surpasses the stage of holophrastic speech, i.e.,
utterances consisting of one word. The one-word utterances
of the infant have a vocative meaning in the case of nouns
and an imperative meaning in the case of verbs. Both cases
refer to a given or desired situation. As soon as the child is
capable of a (diremic) construction, consisting of a subject
and a predicate, he is also able to free himself from his
respective *hic et nunc*. The child becomes aware that he can
assign different activities to the same subject and different
subjects to the same activity. And he begins playing with this
possibility of contextual variations. Children are known to
take great pleasure in untrue and nonsensical utterances such
as "dog meow." They are obviously well aware of the
truth-value of such formulations. They protest when adults,
thinking themselves so tolerant, imitate their constructions.
It is at this stage of linguistic development that the child
discovers his ability to break things up and thus to extract
new aspects from them. This active procedure, of both
destructive and creative potential, enables the child to escape
the narrow bonds of his situation. He learns to make
statements about things which apply only from another,
temporally or spatially divergent or even fictitious, point of
view (1973b:68ff.; 1974c).

The differing choice of terms reveals the divergent
conceptions of the historical situation. For a view other than
one's own familiar one, existential philosophy selected the
negative term, *alienation* (Russian, *otčuždenie;* German,
Entfremdung). Russian formalism introduced the positive

term, *estrangement* (Russian, *ostranenie;* German, *Verfrem-
dung*). For Sartre (1943:525), alienation is not something
that I encounter "in" my situation, enabling me to undertake
the appropriate reshaping of it, but rather something that
befalls me from outside, from others, and that is beyond my
control. The Russian formalists, on the other hand, view
estrangement as a potential device intrinsic to our respective
linguistic systems. Like the child, the poet also makes
destructive and constructive use of this device on all levels of
language. Jakobson (1921a:63) cites Mallarmé's comment
that he offers the bourgeois words that the latter reads in his
newspaper every day, but offers them in a startling context.
He (ibid., 107) also cites Xlebnikov, who interchanges the
initial consonants of words so that their meaning wavers. This
variation of context as well as the overlapping of contrasting
situations as practiced mainly by Brecht, who took the term
estrangement from the formalists (stage direction: Brutus
simultaneously curses Caesar as a tyrant and maltreats a
slave!), are not considered restrictions but rather enrichment,
whereby new perspectives are exposed.

While hermeneutics since Dilthey and Heidegger accord
cardinal importance to the concept of understanding, of
subjective appropriation, structuralism focuses on the term
translation again, as in the old hermeneutics (*hermèneuein* =
to translate). Here again, however, the orientations diverge.
The guiding line of the old hermeneutics is the historical text
in its original context as starting point for textual interpretation. The guiding line of recent hermeneutics is the
subjective horizon of the interpreter himself as starting point
for an appreciation of the ancient text. But the guiding line
of structuralism is the objective possibilities of the linguistic
system. Translation into another context, i.e., even clarifi-
cation of elliptic speech, brings to light manifold actual and
potential relations of the objects referred to. According to
the thesis that Jakobson (1962b:SW II 275) took up from
Peirce, the fundamental trait of the linguistic sign is its
translatability. Every sign can, in principle, be replaced by
another sign. Every sign is translatable into another refer-

ential system which, if not verbalized, is at least verbalizable. In the motion picture industry, scenes at night can be filmed by day through the use of special filters. This procedure is called "day for night" by the English film makers and *nuit américaine* by the French. But there are countless other ways of identifying it. The most striking illustration is Jakobson's own interpretation. In the classical theory of signs as it was developed by the Stoics, the *signans* appears as *perceptibile* and the *signatum* as *intelligibile*. Jakobson translates intelligible into translatable in his own structuralistic system of relations (1965b:SW II 345; see 1959a:SW II 260ff.). With the category of translation, he succeeds in getting an objective, "solid" grasp of the subjective, more elusive category of understanding.

In translation, as in every other domain, structuralism is interested both in what endures, the invariant, and what changes, the variant (1959a:SW II 262). Like estrangement, variation in intra- and interlingual translation is therefore not primarily seen as betrayal (*traduttore—traditore*), but as a new possibility of understanding. This is also how Jakobson interprets the use of tropes and figures of speech in poetry.

> The essence of poetic figures of speech does not simply lie in their recording the manifold relationships between things, but also in the way they dislocate familiar relationships. The more strained the role of the metaphor in a given poetic structure, that much the more decisively are traditional categories overthrown; things are arranged anew in the light of newly introduced generic signs. (1935a:144)

The third characteristic concept of existential philosophy is the concept of world. This concept is not used so much in the classical, philosophical sense of the totality of appearances, but much more in the colloquial sense of designating the personal horizon of a person or class, as in expressions like "my world," "the world of the French," "the world of the laborer," "the professional world," etc. This restriction is symptomatic of the subjective, egocentric attitude of existential philosophy. In contrast, the cultural and theoretical background of structuralism leads to an unequivocal declaration of war from the outset on any and every private or political form of egocentricity. The East European structuralists interpret Husserl's "antipsychologism" as a rejection of individualistic psychology and as an appeal for the sociological, intersubjective elucidation of cultural phenomena (Jakobson, 1929a:SW I 21). In a pamphlet entitled *Evropa i Čelovečestvo*, 1920 ("Europe and Humanity") Trubetzkoy attacked the cultural chauvinism of the Romano-Germanic Occident, which equates Western culture with the culture of humanity. Western ethnocentrism is usually explained by the claim to absolutism in the biblical religions. Trubetzkoy suggests a different historical genesis. In the Roman Empire, the "whole world" (*orbis terrarum*) designated the countries and peoples in the region of the Mediterranean, who had acquired a series of common cultural values through constant traffic with each other. The so-called cosmopolitanism of modern Europe was limited to the adoption of the cultural values of the Greco-Roman *orbis terrarum*. Sartre (1966:88), sharing an East European newspaper cliché of the fifties, called structuralism "the last dam that the bourgeoisie can erect against Marx." If one wishes to argue in the same style, then from the point of view of structuralism one could call the extremely egocentric existential philosophy the last flowering of "Romano-Germanic chauvinism."

2.2. *Object and subject*

2.2.1. *Jakobson's structuralism as Husserlian.* In a discussion with Lévi-Strauss (1963:633), Ricoeur suggested labeling structuralism as "Kantian(ism) without a transcendental subject."* Particularly from the phenomenological side, the

---

*Lévi-Strauss accepts Ricoeur's formula inasmuch as it allows a restrictive interpretation. He rejects two things in particular: first, the existentialistic and personalistic conception of subject, according to which a human being is something that eludes every attempt at scientific determination ("The words 'creator' and 'subject' ... do not embarrass me, if they are devoid of all mysticism"—1973b), and second, the intellectualistic view, according to which languages and myths are the product of reflective acts of thought (1964:19). We

criticism is made that structuralism sacrifices the subject for an impersonal, self-regulating system. The subject, the focus of modern philosophy as the creative source of form and sense in the world, is supplanted by an "absolute formalism," for which only objects and interobjective relations exist. Should this criticism prove applicable, it would indeed be grave. It is directed toward a scientific movement whose model is language, that is, a process which normally involves not merely one, but at least two, subjects. The exclusion of the subjective pole in this context would render almost anyone sceptical.

On closer examination, however, one again finds that what critics consider a failing of structuralism is, in fact, a complex treatment and formulation of the problem. The subject in Jakobson's structuralism appears in three shapes: (1) as observer, who is himself part of the observation; (2) as intersubjective and (3) unconscious producer and recipient of the linguistic message. Instead of being Kantian, in the sense of a philosophy aimed at the a priori and universal forms and laws of its object and without a "transcendental subject," Jakobson's structuralism proves to be Kantian with a more sophisticated concept of the subject. The subject is extended by the dimensions of intersubjectivity and the unconscious. Foucault's "death of the subject" is no motto of Jakobson's; Lacan's formula, the "decentralization of the ego," has more affinity with his thought. But in Jakobson the ego is dethroned for the sake of intersubjectivity as much as for that of the unconscious. Polemics against all political, cultural, or scientific forms of egocentrism are conspicuously frequent in Jakobson and Trubetzkoy and are anchored in a Russian ideological tradition (Jakobson, 1929d:631f.;

---

find the absolutism of Ricoeur's formula misleading, to say the least, for the work of both Lévi-Strauss and Jakobson. It is based on statements which, taken out of context, are ambiguous. It does not do justice to the more comprehensive expositions on the question of the subject, which are not infrequent in Lévi-Strauss (1950: XXVIff.; 1973a: 20ff.). In more recent publications, Ricoeur (1969) has clearly moved in the direction of the structuralist position as regards the dependence of the ego on both the object (language) and the unconscious. However, his striking formula of 1963 continues to enjoy great popularity.

1939c:SW II 505). One of the theses of the *Cercle linguistique de Prague* of 1929 (20) reads:

> *The investigator should avoid egocentrism, i.e., the analysis and evaluation of poetic facts of the past or of other peoples from the point of view of his own poetic habits and of those artistic norms which guided the course of his education.* Moreover, a poetic fact of the past can survive or be resurrected as an active factor in another milieu; it can become an integral component of a new system of artistic values, but at the same time, of course, its function changes and the fact itself undergoes a corresponding modification. The history of poetry must not project this modified fact as such back into the past. On the contrary, it must restore it in its original function, in the framework of the system into which it was born.

The neo-Kantian philosophy that enriched the transcendental subject with the same dimensions was Husserlian philosophy. The Husserlian analysis of the mind leads from the problematic of apperception, via an extremely egologic polarization, to an inclusion of intersubjective and unconscious forms of the constitution in the transcendental problematic. With the exception of the egocentric polarization of the middle phase of Husserl's philosophy, Jakobson's statements on the subject-relatedness of language and literature coincide with the key points of the Husserlian analysis of the mind. It is, therefore, our thesis that Jakobson's structuralism is to be designated Husserlian as regards the question of the subject.

With this thesis, we turn away from the phenomenologists' reception of structuralism in the sixties and toward their much friendlier reception in the thirties. Unlike Ricoeur (1963:33), who fears the rise of a kind of intellectualism which is fundamentally antireflective, anti-idealist, and anti-phenomenological,* the phenomenological interpreters and

---

*Both Jakobson and Lévi-Strauss (1973a:22f.) seek to transcend antagonisms such as reflective and observational, idealistic and materialistic, and phenomenological and naturalistic, and to integrate them into a "total" science in which their results coincide.

reviewers of the thirties (Gurwitsch, 1935:431f.; Pos, 1939a
and b, see Jakobson, 1974e:14f.) were much more inclined
to see a convergence of phenomenology and structuralism.
For Gurwitsch and Pos this convergence lay mainly in the
dual approach to language via observation from the outside
and via the inner and direct experience as participant. Our
thesis additionally rests on the exploration of intersubjective
and unconscious aspects of linguistic creation.

The historical situation can be presented as follows. In
his thesis of the subject as an integral part of everyday
experience and scientific observation, Jakobson has been
directly inspired by Husserl's doctrine of apperception.
Husserl (1913:381) criticizes the old sensualistic doctrine of
apperception, which reduces apprehension to the influx of
additional sensations to those already present. Apperception
must be defined as an act, as a specific interpretation of the
sense material at hand. Similarly, Jakobson (1941:SW I 350)
opposes the attempt to attribute the perception of speech
sounds to certain elementary auditory sensations. Linguistic
perception does not depend on those characteristics which
distinguish speech sounds from other "ordinary" noises, but
only on the "subjective" processing of the raw material of
the senses into linguistic values, its classification* in terms of
the respective language system.

Jakobson's treatment of intersubjectivity has only been
partially and indirectly influenced by Husserl via the above
mentioned interpretation of Husserl's antipsychologism as a
rejection of the individualistic psychological explanation in
favor of a sociological approach. When Husserl visited Prague
in 1935, Jakobson did, however, have the opportunity to
discuss the intersubjective side of language with him personally.

Finally, as far as the question of the unconscious and
involuntary constitution is concerned, a mere convergence is
ascertained. Husserl's manuscripts on this form of creation,
which he headed with the obscure and ambiguous title
"passive genesis" and also with the striking formulation

---

*Marty, in particular, has worked out the classificatory, i.e., systematic, aspect
of apperception (Holenstein, 1972:140ff.).

"constitution without ego-participation," have only in recent years been published more frequently and studied in comparison with the psychoanalytic concept of the unconscious (Holenstein, 1972:192ff., 327ff.).

2.2.2. *The observer as a part of his observation.* As a young student at the University of Moscow in 1915/16, Jakobson took part in two seminars of the psychologist G. J. Čelpanov in which the up-and-coming theses of gestalt psychology and phenomenology were discussed. Jakobson was charged with the treatment of apperception in Steinthal (1871:166ff.) and Husserl (1913:309ff., 563ff.). The starting point of the theory of apperception is the observation that the same objects can apparently be differently apprehended. To use Husserl's favorite illustration, we suddenly grasp as letters the same figures that we first held to be arabesques. The doctrine of apperception concludes that a purely objective investigation is an illusion. The study of an object should be linked with methodological reflection on the orientation, point of view, or mode of apprehension of the subject. A subjective orientation can in principle be modified or exchanged with another orientation. For the same object there is more than one approach and more than one theory.

The subjective problematic has also been formulated independently of Husserl in structuralistic literature. An early statement in Saussure's *Cours* (1916:8) reads, "it is the viewpoint that creates the object." In Jakobson, however, Husserl's influence cannot be ignored, although he avoids the somewhat antiquated expression *apperception* and uses the Husserlian synonyms *Einstellung* ("set") and *Meinung* ("that which is meant"). Later, especially after he met and worked with Niels Bohr, the formulation from quantum physics of the inseparability of observer and object gradually superseded the phenomenological terminology.

The significance of subjective orientation for the formal constitution of an object is especially evident in the two disciplines, poetics and phonology, which Jakobson subjected (together with morphology) to the closest scrutiny.

2.2.2.1. *The set in poetry.* Among the manifold factors

of which a speech event is composed, one in particular appears as the focal point of perception in poetry, namely, the linguistic medium or the message as such.

> The set (*Einstellung*) toward the *message* as such, focus on the message for its own sake, is the *poetic* function of language. (1960b:356)

> In emotional expression passionate outbursts govern the verbal mass, . . . But poetry—which is simply an utterance with a set toward expression—is governed, so to speak, by its own immanent laws; the communicative function, essential to both practical language and emotional language, has only minimal importance in poetry. Poetry is indifferent to the referent of the utterance, while, on the other hand, practical or more exactly object-oriented prose is indifferent to rhythm. (1921a:30)

Jakobson's inclusion of the transcendental, i.e., the subject-oriented, approach is nowhere more apparent than in his treatment of realism, which sees itself as repudiating a subjective view of things in favor of a purely object-oriented approach. This, according to Jakobson (1921b), represents a self-deception. What is considered realistic depends upon the point of view of the person making the judgment, who, as a rule, considers his own viewpoint closest to the truth. Current forms have little appeal for a member of the avant-garde. They ignore aspects of reality that he finds essential. Thus, he deviates from the established canons of artistic endeavor and proclaims his deviation as a more accurate presentation of reality. This applies to the art movements of the nineteenth century, which took realism as their explicit catchword. It is equally applicable to art trends such as symbolism, futurism, and expressionism, which, measured by the criteria of realism as they were canonized in the second half of the nineteenth century, behave most unrealistically. Since the name *realism* had already been claimed, the proponents of the newer trends called themselves realists in a "higher" or "truer" sense of the word. The conservative opposes the revolutionary since he no longer sees his view of the world guaranteed by the new art forms and, consequently, rejects the deformation of the current artistic fashion as a distortion of reality.

2.2.2.2. *The set in phonology.* The subjective dependence of phonology is no less conspicuous. A two-fold change in orientation took place with the rise of phonology. The first concerns turning away from the articulation of sounds, the focus of interest in traditional linguistics, and toward auditive perception.

> Just as questions regarding the tendencies and aims of phonological phenomena have superseded questions regarding the production of sounds, so the physiology of the sounds of language in the role of the interpretation of the external, material aspects of these phenomena has increasingly yielded its top-ranking position to acoustics; it is the acoustic and not the motor image that is meant by the speaking subject and that constitutes the social fact. (1929a:SW I 23)

The second change in orientation involves a shift from the great diversity of sound perception, the focus of traditional phonetics, to those phonic features which exercise a linguistic function as meaning-differentiating elements. Unlike the profusion of phonetic features of sounds, which vary from individual to individual and from situation to situation, the meaning-differentiating features of a language form part of a relatively small universal system of oppositional relations.

To succeed in the sound analysis of a foreign language, it is vital to hit upon the system of these distinctive features and to avoid confusing them with the features which have a prosodic, expressive, or still other function in one's own language. Jakobson (1923:51) recalls that when he first came to Prague, it seemed to him that, because of the regular emphasis on every syllable in Czech, everyone was preaching. It also seemed, as it did to other Russians, that the women in Prague were whining, due to the long qualitative pauses in their speech. The quantitative differences, which exercise a

meaning-differentiating function in Czech, are initially perceived by the Russian as a merely expressive means, as is the
case with his own language.

Music displays an analogous phenomenon. One musical
system builds on the principle of pitch; another on timbre.
Upon hearing an African melody played on two different
instruments, a European thinks he has heard two different
melodies since he concentrates on differences in pitch
between the two renditions. The African, however, assures
him that it is the same melody; for him the timbre, which has
remained identical, is alone decisive.

> What is important in music is not the naturalistic datum, not
> those tones that are realized, but rather those that are *meant.* The
> native and the European hear the same tone and mean completely
> different things with them since they apprehend them in terms of
> two different musical systems; the tone functions in music as a
> tone immanent to the system. The realizations can be manifold;
> the acoustics specialist determines this with precision, but
> musically decisive is that the *piece of music must be recognized as
> identical.* Thus there exists between a musical value and its
> realizations exactly the same relationship as, in language, between
> a phoneme and the sounds that represent this intended phoneme
> in discourse. (1932a:SW II 551f.)

Phonology manifests a remarkable repetition of the
realism problem pointed out in literature by Jakobson. In
phonology the problem is highlighted in the conceptual pair
abstract/concrete. Depending on the point of view, distinctive features and phonemes are seen as abstract, fictitious
constructs of science or, on the contrary, as a repudiation of
scientific constructions and a return to the concrete. Scholars
of traditional phonetics in particular regard the system of
distinctive features only as scaffolding, artificially imposed
upon the profusion of sound variations. According to these
scientists, the principles of phonological elucidation are not
discovered in the object itself, but are rather asserted on the
basis of independent scientific criteria and then tested on the
facts. On the other hand, the Husserlian Aron Gurwitsch

(1935:431f.), in one of the earliest philosophical responses to the new phonology, acclaimed the "turn toward the concrete," i.e., the turn toward the speaker's apprehension and experience of data—a characteristic of the new science which is quite as important as its structuralism and universalism.

> Trubetzkoy [1933] sees in phonology ... above all a symptom or a particular manifestation of a broader scientific movement which extends to many disciplines and of which *structuralism* and *universalism* are the characteristic traits. The *set toward the concrete* seems still more important to us, i.e., the tendency to take things as they are experienced, lived, used, and handled and to rely on the implicit interpretation which is immanent to the use made of them in real life. This tendency effaces the effort that was made to penetrate the supposedly objective reality concealed behind so-called subjective appearance.

Similarly, Sapir (1933) recognized the "psychological reality" of phonemes. A native speaker finds it very difficult to perceive phonetic variants which have no linguistic function. In speaking and listening, he aims exclusively at phonemically relevant units. Therefore, as far as function is concerned, phonic variants not matched with a phonemic unit are fictions for him. Recent investigations in experimental psychology reveal a further shift in point of view. They demonstrate that the listener in average conversation is not aware of the separate distinctive features of phonemes, but does directly perceive morphemes, i.e., their typical properties. They overlook their narrow base. Many distinctive features necessary for identification of an isolated phoneme become redundant in a larger context for the simple reason that in every language rigorous laws of compatibility limit the combination of phonemes. However, the moment perception is impeded, the listener begins to concentrate on features which he usually ignores.

In poetry, with its set toward the message, attention is also drawn to the phoneme and its distinctive features.

The unrivaled works of Velimir Xlebnikov, a versatile explorer in

poetic creation, have opened a vast perspective on the inner
puzzles of language. This artist's search for the "infinitesimals of
the poetic word," his paranomastic play with minimal pairs, or, as
he himself used to say, "the internal declension of words" like
/m,éč/ — /m,áč/, /bík/ — /bók/, /bóbr/ — /bábr/ and such verses
as "/v,íd,il víd,il v,ós,in vós,in,/" (*videl vydel vësen v osen'*)
prompted "the intuitive grasp of an unknown entity," the
anticipation of the **ultimate phonemic units,** as they were to be
called some two decades later. (1962a:SW I 632f.)

This poetic experience of language supplied Jakobson
with the point of departure for his phonological researches
(1921a, 1923). It is always the set that creates the psychical
reality.

2.2.2.3. *The etic and emic points of view.* Although
they recognize phonology as the model discipline of the
structural method, a surprising number of critics of the
structural movement utterly ignore the cardinal role of
subjective orientation in laying bare the phonological system.
Usually the concept of system, the proof that a set of
elements can be determined by a small number of oppositional relations, is alone honored as the unique contribution
of phonology to general scientific methodology. Yet it is
precisely the American structuralists, to whom a crass
positivism is often attributed, who have studied in detail the
subjective factor, brought into play by phonology, in its
import for the groundwork and departmentalization of
scientific research.

On the basis of the antithesis of phonetics and
phonemics, Kenneth Pike (1967:37ff.) distinguishes an *etic*
and an *emic* point of view. The etic sciences approach an
object from the outside. They bring criteria to bear on their
object which are first foreign to it and second of an
unsystematic nature. The emic sciences, on the other hand,
commence with the structures which they have discovered in
the object and which together form a closed system.

In the study of a foreign language, it is the aim of
structural linguistics to bring the initial position of a
cryptanalyst (Jakobson, 1956a:SW I 475f.) who hears a

message but does not have its code at his command closer to the position of a native listener who already possesses the code of the speaker. In studying a language, the code which both speaker and listener utilize unconsciously and unthinkingly must be uncovered. Through arbitrary manipulation and interpretation, the cryptanalyst tries to track down the code in successive stages. His method is similar to the method known as "trial and error" in psychology. The native listener knows from the start which features of the message he must concentrate on and to which categories he must assign each of the elements.

The problem is somewhat more complex than it is sometimes presented by phonologists—in part apparently for didactic reasons. The outside observer is not without a system. His problem is that he tackles the message with a foreign, inappropriate, or wrong code so that his receipt of it is prejudiced from the start. "He will approach the language foreign to him within the framework of his own phonological system, with his own phonological habits; he will so to speak transphonologize this language" (1923:31). This adjustment to the listener's own code is even demonstrable in non-linguistic perceptions of sound.

> Interference by the language pattern affects even our responses to non-speech sounds. Knocks produced at even intervals, with every third louder, are perceived as groups of three separated by a pause. The pause is usually claimed by a Czech to fall before the louder knock, by a Frenchman to fall after the louder; while a Pole hears the pause one knock after the louder. The different perceptions correspond exactly to the position of the word stress in the languages involved: in Czech the stress is on the initial syllable, in French, on the final, and in Polish, on the penult. When the knocks are produced with equal loudness but with a longer interval after every third, the Czech attributes greater loudness to the first knock, the Pole, to the second, and the Frenchman, to the third. (1952a:10f.)

The distortion with which we initially perceive another language is usually accompanied by a disparaging value judgment. In this respect, linguistic perception is no different from any other perception. A farmer from northern Russia, who saw a camel for the first time in his life at an agricultural exposition was incensed (over the evil Communists): "Those scoundrels, look at how they have mutilated that horse!" (1931b:636).

On the other hand, the code of the external observer may be too general. The external observer can be compared not only to a cryptanalyst but also to a temple thief or an iconoclast who has no interest in the work of art as such, but only in the quantity of gold, silver, or other materials. The method of traditional phonetics was not quite as particularistic and atomistic as Trubetzkoy (1933:233f.) portrayed it in comparison with the new. It, too, had a system, but a heterogeneous one. Rather than being specifically linguistic, it was generally physicalistically and physiologically oriented. And it was an eclectic system, whose principles, such as the economic principle of least effort, the physical principle of mechanistic influences on the speech organs, and the psychological principle of analogy, were not hierarchically arranged, but organized *ad hoc* according to the demands of the moment.

Neither can it be claimed that only phonemically relevant features form a system, while features that are not phonemically pertinent to sound perception present an amorphous hodgepodge. At the least, they are subject to the general laws of perception, such as the law of figure and background, the law that similar elements together form a group, and the laws that every element is given in an ascending series—every tone, for instance, appears higher or lower than another tone whether or not the pitch is phonemically relevant—and is given within a chain of more or less contiguous elements.

Inasmuch as system represents the criterion of the emic method, one must concur with Lévi-Strauss (1973a:21) when he states that the nature of things is not etic but emic. There is no such thing as amorphous perception and no totally amorphous formation of theory. As far as the adequacy, the specificity, of a system is concerned, the distinction between an etic and an emic point of view still has a justified claim to validity, which has not received the recognition it deserves. A theory that explains the sentence "Napoleon was a great general" on the basis of a purely statistical explanation of the succession of *was* after *Napoleon* does less justice to the speaker's motivation to use the verb *was* after *Napoleon* than a theory that recurs to an explanation based on a categorial analysis of *Napoleon* and *was*.

2.2.2.4. *The distinction between code and mere metalanguage.* Regarding the question of the observer, Jakobson (1961a:SW II 574f.; 1962b:SW II 276ff.) insists on a distinction put forward in the theory of information by the London school. The physicist receives from nature indices, i.e., signs, that are apprehended as being caused by nature. He translates them into a system of symbols, i.e., signs, whose content is determined by intersubjective convention. Basically, there are several systems which can with validity be applied to the facts of nature. The situation for the linguist is quite different. The object of his investigation is not only the sign but also the code on the basis of which the sender emits his signs. This means that the linguist receives signs that are already determined by convention. The physicist receives no metalinguistic information from his object of research; the linguist does. His "object of research" can comment on its own signs. And the linguist can in turn interfere in the process of information and take over the role of the sender. Unilateral information becomes bilateral communication. The linguist does not seek a theory whose sole criterion is its suitability for the object under observation and its inner consistency. The possible theories of language, known as metalanguages, are characterized by coinciding with the code, the convention, or the metalanguage of the sender himself.

A physicist has to establish agreement between two sets of data: the facts of nature and the system of the theory. A linguist is confronted with three data groups: the message or object language of the sender, the code of the sender, and the metalanguage or theory of the linguist.

With the three fields of reference, code-message-metalanguage, structuralism propounds a synthesis of the logico-positivistic and phenomenological explanations. For the positivistic explanation, the criterion, in addition to observational adequacy (adjustment to the object) and consistency (absence of contradiction), is the greatest possible simplicity of explanatory principles. The additional criterion for phenomenology is its intuitive givenness. Structuralism aims at grasping a thing both from within and without through explanatory means that can be constructed as theoretical artifacts and at the same time disclosed as mental phenomena. The apprehension from within and without must be made to coincide. A structuralistic theory introduces only those constructs that have an intuitive equivalence and admits only those intuitions that can be translated into a corresponding behavioristic or physicalistic construction.

The mental givenness of phonological and semantic features is evident to every speaker insofar as he does not bar his access to it through prejudices about the possibility of the existence of mental entities. But it is always private evidence, which cannot be made directly accessible to a partner. Phonological and semantic features can, however, also be constructed hypothetically without reliance on their subjective givenness. Then, in a second step, the adequacy of the construction is experimentally tested. Thus, the inner availability of semantic features, i.e., the existence of "inner speech," is investigated with the help of comparative stimuli, which have several elementary features in common, and a test stimulus, which shares an important feature with only one of the two comparative stimuli (Cohen et al., 1975:II). As comparative stimuli, a test person is presented with, for example, a June bug and a lady bug, and as test stimulus, a toadstool (fly agaric) or simply the word *toadstool*. The object of the experiment is to test whether normal persons and aphasics associate the word *toadstool* with the comparative stimulus with which it shares the feature "spotted" (i.e., the ladybug), and further, whether this feature is also part of their verbal inventory, their external language, or whether one can and must postulate that it is only part of their mental inventory, their inner language. Jakobson himself practiced this "total," both inner and outer, apprehension of a phenomenon mainly in phonology. The distinctive features are defined perceptually and, at the same time, acoustically/physiologically. The inner experience can be translated into the terminology of outer experience and conversely.

2.2.3. *The intersubjective constitution of language.* Far from eliminating from science the relation to the subject, structuralism seeks to differentiate the forms of subjective constitution of objects. The structuralistic reflection on the subject is a reaction to the thesis of the neogrammarians "that language is not a thing which leads a life of its own outside of and above human beings, but that it has its true existence only in the individual, and hence that all changes in the life of a language can only proceed from the individual speaker" (Osthoff and Brugmann, 1878:204). The manifesto of the neogrammarians objects "that people always said 'language' when, strictly speaking, they ought to have said 'the men who speak'—it was not, for example, the Greek language which was averse to spirants, dropped final *t*, changed *thíthēmi* to *títhēmi*, etc., but those among the Greeks with whom the sound change in question started. . . ." (ibid., 209). This thesis of the individual as the sole vehicle of language and the sole source of linguistic change in turn represents a reaction to the mythologizing hypostases of romantic theories of language. Romantics considered language a kind of living organism, which evolves according to biological laws and which is animated by "the soul of the people."

Structuralism shares the goal of a strictly scientific linguistics with the neogrammarians, but not the procedure in attaining this goal. The neogrammarian means of "demythologization" are individualization and psychologization; the means of structuralism, formalization of language and sociologization of its subject. Language is viewed not as an organism but as a system, and the vehicle of language is no longer the soul of the people but an intersubjective community. For the neogrammarians, the physical and psychical nature of the individual is the sole substrate of language and the only real mode of appearance. Language as an objective and hence supraindividual system of general forms and laws is lost. The entire dispute involving romanticism, neogrammarianism, and structuralism takes place once again under the heading of realism. Structuralism opposes the thesis "that individual language alone is the real language" (1929c:SW IV 1) and that all else is reduced to either a mythological hypostasis or a scientific construct.

The originality of Jakobson's conception can best be highlighted in contrast to that of Husserl. Husserl's explication of intersubjectivity has something contemplative about it, like all of his philosophy. He sets out from the objects of nature. A thing that I perceive appears not only in relation to me as the subject of perception and as the pole of the perspective in which it is given; it also refers to other subjects, to whom it appears in another perspective from another standpoint. Another person's "view of the world" is not simply a duplicate of my own. Our views of the world are not congruent, they are asymmetric. Herein consists, for Husserlian phenomenology, the advantage of the intersubjective view of the world.

The intersubjective givenness of things is, however, also the basis for their suitability as signs, as means of communication. It is at this stage that Jakobson intervenes. The concern is no longer mere contemplation of the objects of nature but communication and exchange of cultural objects. Thus, terms that appear not at all or only marginally in Husserl step to the fore, economic and political terms such as *supply* and *demand, censorship* and *sanction.* The last mentioned calls to mind the key term in the Hegelian treatment of intersubjectivity: *recognition.* Intersubjective experience resembles economic or legal commerce.

Together with Petr Bogatyrev, Jakobson explored the

intersubjective constitution of linguistic products, especially in the field of folklore (1929c:SW IV 1ff.). The objective existence of a literary work, i.e., an existence that endures and is available to anyone, is basically assured with its written fixation. An oral folkloric work, however, depends for its existence on acceptance by a community. Only those elements of form and content which have been accepted by the community outlive their author. Our formulation must be still more precise. Social sanctions do not affect a folkloric work after it has been created. They do not affect the "supply" of the individual folkloric poet but rather exercise a kind of preventative censorship. The creation of folklore arises out of a collective "demand" as regards narrative patterns and models for plots which are acceptable to the community. The code to which the folkloric poet is attuned appears in the form of censorship. Literary works are subjected to a subsequent censorship when, in a second phase of their existence, they have gone down as "degraded cultural values" in the folklore of a social milieu to which they were not originally addressed.

Analogous intersubjective components are also manifested in more common linguistic facts. A sound change differs from a mere lapsus in that it is adopted and sanctioned by society, guardian of the currently operative code (1929c:SW IV 2). The point of departure for Jakobson and Bogatyrev's argumentation is Saussure's definition of *langue* as that which bears "the stamp of collective approval" (1916:15).

The relationship between individual and intersubjective communication partially overlaps with the relationship between creation and diffusion. Jakobson's thesis asserts that the two latter notions cannot be separated. An undisseminated linguistic creation is indistinguishable from a lapsus. Only a validating reception raises it above an ordinary slip of the tongue. The emergence of a creation does not depend upon the subjective source and the psychological motivation, but only upon recognition through acceptance, be it active or passive repetition or transferral to analogous cases. Even a misprint can, if received with approbation, become a creation. The Russian poet Xlebnikov acclaimed the artistic potential of misprints (Jakobson, 1921b:35).

Purely private creation and diffusion, restricted to the personal code of an individual, are also feasible. In a discussion of Saussure's dichotomy *langue/parole,* Jakobson (1939a:SW I 285) opposes equating it with the juxtaposition of supraindividual social products and individual private property. Every speaker gradually creates his own linguistic idiosyncrasies, his individual norms, and his personal style.

2.2.4. *The unconscious constitution of language.* Unconscious constitution is a widespread thesis not restricted to structuralism alone. It plays a cardinal role in the old neogrammarian linguistics as well as in the latest generative and transformational linguistics. In connection with this theme, Jakobson usually refers to a letter of September 30, 1876, from the young Kruszewski to Baudouin de Courtenay:

> "I don't know what it is that attracts me to linguistics like a magnet unless it is the unconscious character of the forces of language. Actually, I have only just now noticed that you always add the expression *bessoznatel'nyi* 'unconscious' when you list these forces. I find this most interesting because it touches upon an idea that has been going round in my mind for some time, namely the idea of an unconscious process in general, an idea which [through its logical conception] radically diverges from the thought of [the romantic philosopher, Eduard von] Hartmann." (cited by Jakobson, 1965a:SW II 431)

In spite of its prevalence, the question of an unconscious creation of cultural objects is difficult to resolve. The lack of methodologically clarified possibilities of access has repeatedly led to fallacious attempts at solution. We can, therefore, do little more than present a few preliminaries on this theme in the light of material explored by Jakobson and suggestions he has brought forward in this respect.

In recent publications, Jakobson (see 1970a) uses the expression *subliminal* instead of the classical term *uncon-*

scious to safeguard an important distinction. To begin with,
two forms of consciousness must be distinguished: the
reflective, theming consciousness, i.e., the deliberate and
rational process of taking cognizance, and a blurred intuitive
inkling which normally remains latent and operates in the
"background or underground of consciousness" but to which
we can direct our attention at any time. We must now
distinguish from this mental unconsciousness those processes
to which introspection has no access, biological and chemical
processes in the brain cells and other organs. The unconscious, in the mental or phenomenological sense, is everything that can be grasped intuitively through reflection, albeit
over great resistance or severe self-deception; this is the case
by definition in the unconscious that is dealt with in
psychoanalysis. All is unconscious, in the physical sense, that
can only be observed from the outside, i.e., the biological
processes of the body and, further, all the physical processes
of nature.

Since introspection leaves much room for deception, it
is far from easy to determine whether the ordered nature of
linguistics represents an unconscious reality in the mental or
physical sense. One must guard against premature constructions. The neogrammarians understood the unconscious
unfolding of language development as a confirmation of their
thesis that language development obeys mechanical laws
(Putschke, 1969:34f.). The neo-Cartesians among linguists
today recur to an innate disposition for every unconscious
performance. We shall demonstrate by the Cartesian example
of the idea of the triangle the fallacies that can result (see
Chomsky, 1966:68f.).

When presented with Figure 3(a), we spontaneously
enlarge it to the triangle in 3(c) and not to a fanciful
construction as in Figure 3(b). A Cartesian explains this fact
by the idea of the triangle, alleged to be innate to man. It is,
however, most doubtful that the human mind is endowed
from birth with such a specific idea as that of the triangle.
With a view to the discoveries of gestalt psychology, we recur
to much simpler and more general dispositions, which also

have a much greater chance of coinciding with the intuition
of a large number of test persons. The laws of gestalt
psychology applicable here are the principle of the closedness
of a figure and the tendency of regular lines to extend in the
imagination with the same regularity beyond the sensorily
perceived end points. Similarly, in complementing Figure
3(d) to Figure 3(f) and not to Figure 3(e), we fall back on
the law of symmetry in gestalt perception.

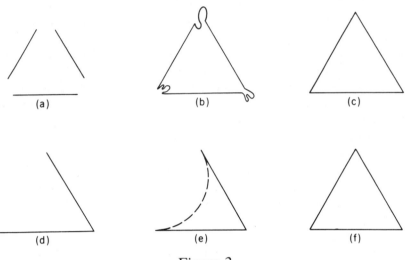

Figure 3

   Jakobson often speaks of the parallels between linguistic
structures and biological and physical structures. He com-
pares Xlebnikov's tendency to repeat sounds five times with
the striking incidence of pentagons in such varied things as
flowers and the bubbles in froth (1970a:303f.). The Russian
poet himself draws comparisons with the five fingers and the
similar structure of the starfish. But what most moves
Jakobson to postulate a biological foundation of linguistic
competence is the extraordinary parallels between the structure of language and of genes (1974e:45ff.; 1974b).

We may state that among all the information-carrying systems, the genetic code and the verbal code are the only ones based upon the use of discrete components, which, by themselves, are devoid of inherent meaning but serve to constitute the minimal senseful units, i.e., entities endowed with their own, intrinsic meaning in the given code. (1974e:50)

Moreover, both systems display a binary and strictly hierarchical arrangement of parts. Binary, oppositional features characterize both individual phonemes and the "letters" of the genetic code. And every partial whole is in each case integrated in a higher unit according to strict "syntactic" laws, analogous to the way in which a word is integrated in a sentence and thus endowed with its specific meaning and function.

With all these striking parallels, one must not lose sight of the methodological distinction upon which Jakobson insisted in the early thirties. At that time, the Prague linguists were fascinated by isolines, which had been discovered among languages, the climate (the isotherms of winter), geographic formations (congruence of linguistic and geographical maps of the north Asian mainland), and a series of cultural phenomena.

Mr. Jakobson recognizes the vast usefulness of the confrontation of linguistic, anthropological, physico-geographical, and cultural isolines. One discovers the most extraordinary congruencies. Thus, the zone of palatalization of consonants is identical to the zone of the five-tone scale, as Trubetzkoy has pointed out. Science must confront, but must not deduce, the facts of one level from those of another. (CLP, 1931a:301)

A causal or functional derivation cannot be undertaken until the confrontation has advanced enough to yield a theory of foundation which proves to be neither too wide nor too narrow. A biological foundation of linguistic competence will not become cogent until those linguistic relations which appear exclusively with certain biological data have been successfully identified and until the modifications on one level correspond to those on the other in an ordered relation.

The old intellectualistic philosophers and psychologists—Husserl no less than Wundt—inclined to accord the unconscious only certain relatively primitive, or what was thought to be primitive, formations. In the cognitive domain, this meant above all associations which exist among different data based on formal relations (similarity, contiguity). All logical activity (categorial explication, classification, valuation) based on the logical and categorial meaning of an object was reserved to reason and the reflective conscious. According to these authors, the unconscious was only secondarily capable of rational activity, namely, when logical operations that were originally performed in the full light of consciousness had become automatic through constant repetition.

Structuralism disclaims such an intellectualistic dualism. The child's acquisition of grammar, in particular, points toward the ability of the unconscious to perform rationally. Without a grasp of categories and categorial connections, the child could not select precisely those parts of the complex discourse of adults which enable him to understand the core. And without categorial understanding, the child with his stock of words could develop no new, original, and meaningful combinations. Not only reason but also the unconscious is categorially structured.

Jakobson's analyses of poems, which beyond semantic sense and phonological form also take into account grammatical relations, the arrangement of morphological and syntactic categories and their relation of parallelism or opposition to the phonological and metric structure of the poem, have met with vehement disapproval from conservative critics. With scepticism or mere rhetoric questions are raised: "Does the reader even notice the relations that are the joy of the investigator?" (cited by Jakobson, 1973a:500). Is the ordered distribution of word categories such as pronouns and adverbs something that springs from the unconscious, creative energy of the poet and appeals to a more or less latent intuition of the reader? Are we not here dealing with subsequent constructions of the structuralistic interpreter?

Recent investigations of pathological speech disorders suggest that the proponents of structural analysis come much closer to the subjective experience of language than the advocates of feeling, who claim the feeling evoked by poems eludes all rational and scientific analysis. They suggest that word categories are not just a linguistic or logical construction but, on the contrary, represent a subliminal, psychical reality, which affects reading and even misreading.

> We presented *Es* 'it' to the patient, and, unable to read it, she said "one of these horrible little words again," whereas she read the little word *Ei* 'egg' without any hesitation. Thus behavior shows quite clearly an additional, very interesting phenomenon, viz. that the patient, in spite of her failure to read it, has somehow grasped that the presented word *Es* is a pronoun. The same phenomenon is brought up by the striking fact that the high percentage of misreadings (66% vs. 7% failure) in the case of pronouns remains to a very high extent within the category of pronouns. Thus she reads *unser* 'our' instead of *euer* 'your' and vice versa. In general, 77% of the misreadings were pronouns, 12% were the copula *ist* (which she seemed to use as a kind of "category indicator"), 8% other grammatical words (auxiliaries and prepositions) and only 2% major lexical categories. Attempting an explanation of these observations forces one to recognize a series of rather complicated steps in the process of understanding written words, beginning with a preliminary subliminal identification of the underlying graphemic pattern (or phonemic . . .), which must be stored for further processing. . . . (Weigl and Bierwisch, 1970:12)

If a word category such as the pronoun underlies the disrupted linguistic performance of a patient suffering from alexia, we may safely assume that such categories are also at work as effective and palpable factors in the production and reception of poetic texts, in which author and reader are attuned to the linguistic medium as such.

2.3. *Form and substance*

According to Derrida (1967:24f., 78ff.; 1968:136ff.), Saussure's historical merit lies in having laid the foundation for a "desubstantialization" of *signifiant* and *signifié*. He finds, however, that Saussure does not go far enough with his "reduction of sound substance" and therefore still remains shackled by the metaphysical tradition of the Occident. Saussure (1916:118) expressly states that the essence of the linguistic *signans* is not phonic, yet he links it up with the *phoné*. It is given to us primarily as an "acoustic image." Derrida further concludes that a *"concept signifié* existing in itself," an absolute *intelligible,* which does not itself act again as *signifiant,* is concealed in Saussure's dichotomy of *signifiant* and *signifié*. Jakobson is included in this "historico-philosophical" critique.

On the other hand, structuralism is accused of leveling the semantic stratum of language and allowing the sense of a linguistic message to be absorbed by its phonological and grammatical form.

We shall try to delineate Jakobson's approach to "form and substance"* and "form and meaning"† first in the realm of phonology and then in that of semantics. Regarding Derrida's critique, it may be said in advance that as far as questions implying an ontological commitment are concerned, Jakobson pays no heed whatsoever to conformity with the philosophical or indeed theological tradition of the Occident or with a fashionable or messianic proclamation of the end of such a tradition. The sole criterion is the matter at hand, in this case, language. Agreement with historical or contemporary trends is welcome as confirmation and is cited with gratification, but it is not essential.

2.3.1. *The role of phonic material.* The old linguistics defined the speech sound according to its positive sensory qualities. Baudouin de Courtenay and Saussure replaced the material definition with a functional and structural one. Phonetics as a natural science was displaced or rather supplemented by phonology as a science of function and form. Linguistics is not indiscriminately interested in all and

---

Form und Substanz, title of the Festschrift in honor of E. Fischer-Jørgensen (see Jakobson, 1970b:SW I 751f.).

†*Form und Sinn,* title of a German collection of articles by Jakobson (1974a).

any material qualities or variations of qualities, but exclusively in those that exercise a meaning-differentiating function. A phonic element cannot display a meaning-differentiating function unless it is itself distinct from other elements which also have such a function. Hence, phonology aims not at positive, absolutely defined qualities, nor at just any differences between qualities, but alone at those differences that distinguish one meaning-differentiating element from another. The distinction between a simple *t* and an aspirated *t* in Russian does not differentiate meaning, but the distinction between a simple *t* and a palatalized *t* does. In aspiration, but not in palatalization, Russian allows the speaker broad play in material variation.

Jakobson's most important contribution to phonology lies in the delimitation of the structure and number of phonic distinctions which have a meaning-differentiating function. The fruit of his endeavor is a hierarchical system of a small number of binary oppositions, which always represents only a fraction of the number of phonemes in a given language. The thirty-six phonemes of the French language are differentiated by only six oppositions of distinctive features. The analysis of features enables us to reduce the profusion of possible alternatives to a small number. If the Czech *l*, which can occur in the same positions as the remaining thirty-two phonemes of this language, could not be broken down still more, then its distinction from the other thirty-two phonemes would demand relations beyond analysis. Its division into three features—vocalic, consonantal, and continuant—reduces its relation to the other phonemes to three binary selections. The identification of a phoneme is greatly simplified. The theory of distinctive features presents an economic advantage, only possible thanks to the orientation of the Prague linguists toward the phonic nature of phonemes and not merely toward their distribution, to which the Danish and a large group of American structuralists had restricted themselves (Ivić, 1965:53).

Distributional analysis rests on the remarkable observation that in every language strict laws govern the succession of phonemes. Not every phoneme can be found in the company of every other phoneme. Two sounds of which one can appear only where the other cannot, in other words, sounds which manifest a complementary distribution, are considered variants of the same phoneme, while two sounds that can alternate in some contexts but not in others are considered different phonemes. Distributional analysis is not only less economical than the analysis of features; it cannot do without an avowed or unavowed recourse to a phonic determination of features.

> The confrontation of the syllables /ku/ and /ki/ does not authorize us to assign both initial segments to one phoneme /k/ as two variants appearing to their mutual exclusion before two different vowels, unless we have identified the common features, unifying the retracted and advanced variety of the phoneme /k/ and differentiating it from all the other phonemes of the same language. Only by means of such a test are we able to decide whether the retracted [k-] in /ku/ implements the same phoneme as the advanced [k+] in /ki/ and not the advanced [g+] in /gi/. (1956a:SW I 474)

> Attempts to identify a phonemic category on the basis of distributional rules alone unavoidably result in an impasse. One cannot, for instance, cite as the primary phonemic definition of the Polish voiced obstruents the fact that they are limited to non-final positions, any more than one could define a dining car as the car in a train which is never found between two freight cars. In order to state that diners or voiced obstruents do not appear in a given position, we must first and foremost know how to identify diners and distinguish them from freight cars, coaches, and Pullmans, or voiced from voiceless obstruents. (1962a:SW I 639)

The hope of having achieved an exclusively formal analysis through distributional analysis is an illusion.

The point is not to abandon a flat orientation toward substance for the sake of an equally flat orientation toward form, but rather to bridge the juxtaposition of form and substance. Phonology teaches that not only sensory qualities are perceived, but also nonsensory, formal qualities such as likeness, difference, and opposition. In identifying a phoneme, we are guided not by a sensory quality, but by an oppositional relation between sensory qualities. We ask, "Did you say *ma* or *pa*?" concentrating on the contrast between nasal and nonnasal when we say or hear the initial consonants of both words.

Form and substance mutually imply each other. In his "structuralistically fundamental meditation," Husserl (1913: 466, 476) submits color/extension and tone-quality/tone-intensity as model illustrations of reciprocal foundedness. Extension or intensity without a material correlate (not substrate) or vice versa is unimaginable. Differences are either directly material in nature (red-green, vocalic-nonvocalic) or refer to those features which can only occur in material elements. Only sensory phenomena such as colors or tones can be dark or light.

The phonic material at the disposal of the child in the babbling stage is not taken over by language *tale quale* with all existing forms and only with existing forms. The linguistic activity absorbs the phonic material by classifying, selecting, and adapting it in terms of its function. Natural phonic material displays a profusion of the most diverse variations, from which linguistic activity extracts binary oppositions or upon which it imposes them. Phonic material as it appears in language is always a "cultural artifact" (Jakobson, 1949a:SW I 423).

In the polemics against material, phonic, and psychological remnants in the phonology of Saussure and Jakobson, two things are generally confounded: (1) the separation of phonology, as a linguistically oriented science of form and function, from phonetics, as a natural science, and (2) the hierarchical arrangement of the various levels of the realization of linguistic signs. If a "psychologizer" (see Derrida, 1968:139f.) is someone who takes the auditive-perceptual level of sound realization as the point of departure for his study of linguistic signs, then Saussure and certainly Jakobson are indeed "psychologizers." Such criticism, however, overlooks the fact that the emphasis on sound perception is not "metaphysically" based. At most, one can speak of a metaphysical dogma in the old psychology of sound, according to which the perceived qualities of sound merely represent an epiphenomenon of "sounds as such," as they are palpably manifested in acoustic waves. Jakobson bases the priority of the perceptual or psychological level on structural and functional grounds. The perceptual level is the level intended by the speaker in normal communication and the level toward which the listener is oriented as well. However, in comparison to the other levels of sound realization, the neurological, acoustic, and articulatory, it is also the most precise and least redundant, for which reason it serves as the starting point for analysis of the different levels (3.4. below).

This priority for the perceptual level applies to written language as well, from a genetic, structural, and functional point of view. Genetically—both individually and socially—spoken language everywhere precedes written language. Audible speech is the most universal, autonomous, and fundamental means of communication. In relation to language, visual signs are throughout substitutive in nature, as in writing, or supplementary, as in gesture (1964a:SW II 334). Phonemes and letters do not have the same sign structure. Phonemes have no uniform, positive, and constant meaning. They merely signalize otherness (*altérité*). The phoneme /d/ in *dollar* signalizes that the word of which it is a part must be distinguished from a word (*collar*) that contains another phoneme (/k/) in the same position. That the phoneme /d/ also occurs in *dull* implies no common ground in syntactic form or semantic content between the two words *dollar* and *dull*. The letter *d,* on the other hand, has a uniform, positive, and constant meaning. It stands for the same thing in every word, namely, the phoneme /d/, although the constant value can, as in English, be restricted by various conventional rules. The functional distinction between phonemes and letters is also reflected in their structure.

Letters never fully reproduce the different distinctive features on which the phonemic pattern is based and unfailingly disregard the structural relationship of these features. (1956a:SW I 475)

Hjelmslev's (1943) postulate that the phonological form can be completely separated from the phonetic material is based on the fallacious supposition that, in language, form is related to matter as a constant to its variables.

> It is no more possible to state that linguistic form is manifested in two equipollent substances—graphic and phonic—than to maintain that musical form is manifested in two variables—notes and sounds. For just as musical form cannot be abstracted from the sound matter it organizes, so form in phonemics is to be studied in relation to the sound matter which the linguistic code selects, readjusts, dissects and classifies along its own lines. (1956a:SW I 475)

The inner structure of phonic and graphic elements is not the same.

There are structures that are indisputably based on matter. Certain structures are valid for each and every kind of object. Every object is in some way either similar to or different from other objects; every object can act as a substrate of attributes and a subject of predicates. Other structures are bound to the nature of their objects. Extension, for example, is a form that is defined by matter. In the literal, nonmetaphorical sense, only material bodies are extended. The structures defined by the concrete nature of objects cannot be isomorphically represented by any object at random, in contradistinction to the most general structures, which are applicable to every object.

Relations may be materially founded from another point of view as well. Herbart (1824:324ff.) observed that properties belonging to the same quality continuum are not characterized by the same relationships as those belonging to different continua. Properties of the same continuum manifest the idosyncracy that they can both blend and repress each other in the same element. Light and dark can mix and blend into an intermediate degree of lightness. On the other hand, a sound, in relation to another particular sound, cannot be light and dark at the same time, while a sound (e.g. [p])

certainly can be simultaneously dark and diffuse. Properties belonging to different continua can be compatible and can enter into "complications."

Jakobson focused on the study of the characteristic distinctions between visual and auditory sign systems (1964a and b:SW II 334ff.). Visual sign systems are dominated by signs caused by their object and implying its co-presence (indexes) and by signs similar to their object and representing it (icons). Furthermore, visual signs are easily reified. There is an involuntary tendency to change them into natural objects. The same people who are unable to relate to abstract art do not even appear to be aware of the absence of reference to reality in music, which is no less abstract. The spatial dimension takes precedence in vision, and the temporal in audition. Still more characteristic is the rigorously hierarchical and granular structure of sound sequences. Music and language are based upon discontinuous, discrete components. None of the visual arts commands such a consistently hierarchical stratification. Jakobson suspects that abstract films are so tiring due to their lack of such compulsory requirements.

2.3.2. *The role and form of meaning.* According to Lévi-Strauss (1963:637), "Sense always results from the combination of elements which are not meaningful in themselves." In the wake of such statements, Foucault (1966) suggests that meaning is "nothing but a kind of superficial effect, a mirage, a froth." One could hardly imagine Jakobson making statements of this kind.

Expression and meaning are the two correlative sides, which cannot be reduced to each other, of every linguistic sign. Meaning is not so much the product of a certain arrangement of expressive elements as the factor responsible for launching a rigorously organized arrangement of vehicles for expression. Nor is it an epiphenomenon whose laws are founded in another reality. Such a statement could only provoke grave misgivings about the methodological postulate of structuralism, i.e., that every field of objects is *primo loco* subject to specific, immanent laws. Meaning and structure or system cannot be played against each other as opposing concepts. Meaning itself is structured and always appears in a system of meaning-combinations and meaning-modifications.

2.3.2.1. *Meaning as a principle of form.* Audible speech does not originate with connections among meaningless elements, out of which sense subsequently emerges or which are subsequently charged with sense. On the contrary, it originates with connections among sounds endowed with their unique linguistic function through recourse to a meaning function, without which they cannot even be defined. The beginnings of language in the proper sense of the word are preceded by a babbling stage, in which the infant is capable of producing all conceivable sounds. In the transition to the first stage of speech, he loses almost his entire inventory of sounds. Step by step he then builds up an artificial system of sounds according to rigorous laws of foundedness interlocked by oppositional features. Certain sounds such as sibilants and liquids, produced effortlessly by the babbling infant, can only be recovered after the acquisition of a complex hierarchy of other sounds.

The stability, the selection of sounds, and the hierarchical stratification of the sound system after the transition from babbling to speaking can only be explained by the new function of the sounds. Babbling satisfies the emotional and motor needs of the infant. The child's babbling is self-contained, egocentric, and not object-related, while speech sounds are characterized by their intention toward meaning and their social orientation. They serve as a means of designation and communication. Those phonic elements are chosen which contribute to the distinction of meanings within a system (1941:SW I 337ff.).

2.3.2.2. *The form of meaning.* The formulation "form and meaning" is foreshortened and as such easily leads one astray. It can give rise to the impression that a linguistic element has a phonological form and, in the case of higher level elements, a grammatical form as well, and, moreover, a meaning, which is itself beyond all formal determinations. This misses the mark. A meaning is not something that eludes

all scientific endeavor, that can only be felt and "intuited."
It, too, is structured and consequently always something that
can be "understood." It can be broken down into its
components. It can be placed in relation to the transformations permitted by its grammatical and semantic structure
and in relation to other meanings to which it is opposed and
together with which it forms a system of meanings. Thus,
enlarging upon the elliptical formulation above, we have
"phonological form, grammatical form, and semantic form."
However, this formulation still leaves room for improvement.
It implies that the meanings in language form a level beside
other levels which can be isolated from each other. Meaning
is encountered on all levels, but its structure is different for
each of them. Thus, meanings that are expressed in the
grammatical form of a word are characteristically distinct
from meanings expressed through a word of their own,
through an independent lexical unit.

Meanings expressed in grammar cannot be omitted; they
are compulsory. Lexical meanings, on the other hand, are
voluntary. They do not have to be expressed. If, for example,
the verbs of a language contain no information about the
time of an action, then a resultant ambiguity can be remedied
by an additional word.

In my opinion the significance of the categorized grammatical
meanings for the cultural behavior of any given speech community should not be minimized. The compulsory character of
these categories, as pointed out by Boas, is of consequence....
When speaking English, I am obliged to reveal whether I go to the
friend or to a friend, while in Russian, devoid of articles, I can,
but need not, expose this distinction. The grammatical pattern
creates a hierarchy of items on which we are supposed to focus
our attention.... In jest, in rhetoric, in poetry, in dreams, in
magic, in what I should call everyday verbal mythology, the
grammatical categories carry a high semantic import. Even such a
category as grammatical genders, often cited as particularly
formalized, plays a great role in the attitudes of the speech
community possessing them. In Russian the feminine cannot
denote a male person, and the masculine cannot specify a female

person. The ways of personification and metaphoric interpretation of inanimate nouns are strongly indicated by their
gender. When as a child I read a German fairy tale in Russian
translation, it seemed absurd to me that Death, obviously a
woman, was represented as an old man, since "death," masculine
in German, is feminine in Russian. A test in the Moscow
Psychological Institute showed that Russians with an inclination
to personify the days of the week, inevitably represented
Monday, Tuesday, and Thursday as males and Wednesday,
Friday, and Saturday as females, without realizing that this is
induced by the masculine gender of the former three against the
feminine gender of the latter three. The difference in the Friday
ritual within the folk tradition of different Slavic peoples is
promoted by the difference in gender of this calendar term. The
widespread superstition that a fallen knife announces a male guest
and a fork a female one is impelled by the masculine of "knife"
and the feminine of "fork" in Russian. Since Russian has no
copula of present tense, the formula *Deus bonus est; ergo Deus
est* loses its point in Russian, and hence the efficacy of this
argument was vitiated in Russian theology. (1953d:279f.; cf.
1959c:SW II 492)

An important distinction in tracking down the inner
structure of a meaningful unit is that between general and
contextual meaning. To illustrate Jakobson's procedure, we
select one of the most frequently analyzed words of
contemporary semantics, the word *bachelor* (1973b:49f.).
Depending on the context, *bachelor* can take on different
meanings: (1) an adult person, but unmarried; (2) a holder of
an academic degree, but the lowest; (3) a knight, but without
a banner of his own; (4) a fur seal, but without mate during
breeding time. The context in which the word is used
transmits the selection of the meaning in question, which is
correspondingly called a contextual meaning. Common to all
four usages are certain invariant features which prevent
bachelor from being considered a homonymous word (as
bank is, which can designate a financial institution as well as
an accumulation of earth or sand along a river or lake). In all
four cases *bachelor* is a noun whose object has the marker

"animate." It cannot be replaced by the pronoun *it,* but in all four cases by the pronoun *he*. In all four contexts, *bachelor* is an adult, but not necessarily a male adult. In the first two meanings, it can also be applied to females, as in "She is a bachelor of arts" or "These houses are for bachelors." The two invariant markers "animate" and "adult" do not suffice, however, to distinguish the meaning of *bachelor* from the meaning of other words. They are not specific enough. In all four cases, *bachelor* is someone who is incomplete in one aspect. The invariant general meaning common to all four is that "they are all adult beings with an incomplete career."

The open class of nouns does not provide the most rewarding access to the study of the system of meaningful units in a language. Far more rewarding are the closed classes of words such as prepositions and pronouns. The more closed a class is the more structured it appears and the more transparent are the laws upon which it is constituted. The most rigorous structuralization is displayed by grammatical meanings, which attain to expression through morphological means.

As a model illustration of the structural analysis of a closed system of meanings, Jakobson's studies on the general meanings of Russian cases (1936b:SW II 23ff.; 1958a:SW II 154ff.) have had a decisive influence on contemporary semantic research (cf. Bierwisch, 1967a:4). In a first step, the invariant meaning of a case is identified. This step is in turn motivated, on the one hand, by the multiplicity of contextual meanings in each of the cases, and, on the other, by the overlapping of contextual meanings from one case to another. Thus, the Russian accusative is used for the direct object of a transitive verb, for the temporal and spatial modifiers of intransitive verbs, for the object of certain prepositions in connection with verbs of movement, and so on. But the direct object of a negated verb can also, though not always, appear in the genitive, and the time modifier in the instrumental.

Just as the phonological system can be subdivided into a system of relations among phonemes and a system of distinctive features, so too can the case system be divided into a system of relations among cases and a corresponding system of case features. The variations and overlappings of the cases can be elucidated by analyzing the case features, which act as the vehicle for the general meaning of the case.

The invariant meaning of the accusative can be pinpointed in its directedness. The book is the target of the reading process in the sentence *ja čitaju knigu* ("I am reading a book"). The sentence *on rabotaet den' i noč'* ("He works day and night") indicates that all the time is consumed by work. The instrumental case behaves differently. It is used when the action does not cover the entire span of time. Time is involved only marginally. Characteristic of the instrumental is the marginal role of the additional entity. *Rabotaet noč'u* ("He works nights") simply means that the work takes place by night and not by day, but not that the whole night is consumed by work. Similarly, in *švyrjat' kamnjami* ("to throw (with) stones" [instrumental]), the accent is not on the stones, but on the throwing, in contradistinction to *švyrjat' kamni* ("to throw stones" [accusative]).

Four Russian cases (nominative, accusative, instrumental, dative) can be placed in a systematic relation to each other through the two core meanings of directedness and marginality. They entertain a relationship of opposition formed by the relation of presence vs. absence of one of the two marks. Thus the nominative is distinguished from the other three cases through the absence of both marks vs. the variable presence of the marks in the other cases. The accusative is opposed to the nominative by the presence of directedness vs. its absence; to the instrumental by the same relation *plus* the absence of marginality vs. its presence; to the dative, which is characterized by both directedness and marginality, by the absence of marginality vs. its presence.

With only one additional feature, quantification, the other two cases in Russian, the genitive and locative, or the other four cases, if one considers the subdivisions of the genitive and locative as independent cases, can be accounted for in a systematic network of opposing relations. A cube whose corners represent the eight cases graphically demonstrates the marking of the individual cases and their oppositional structure (see Jakobson, 1958a:SW II 175; Sangster, 1970:151).

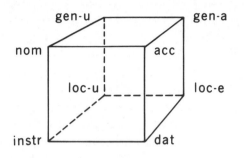

Figure 4

The cases on the right side of the cube share the mark of directedness, those on the bottom the mark of marginality, and those on the back quantification.

Husserl was made famous by his theory of eidetic abstraction, aimed at uncovering the invariant essential traits of an object or a meaning. In the process, he came to the conclusion that extrication of the consistently invariant features of a single object did not suffice to characterize it fully. It must additionally be placed in relation first to the objects of the category or region to which it belongs and then to the totality of categories, to the world in its entirety. This insight largely remained only a postulate in Husserl. His eidetic analyses are atomistically restricted to single objects. The invariant network of relations, within which each object is constituted, remained largely unstudied. Herein lies Jakobson's contribution to eidetic phenomenology, as it is called, which seeks to uncover the eidetic universalities of an object or a region of objects. Jakobson succeeded in demonstrating how a range of objects can be described by a harmonious system of relational features. The cosmos of ideas is no hodgepodge of data that can only be "savored" individually. It is a well-ordered system.

2.3.2.3. *Meaning as a factor of form in poetic texts.* In the struggle against the symbolists' thematic definition of poetry, the Russian futurists and formalists originally promoted phonic matter to the sole object of poetry. "The word as such," unimpeded by a symbolic relation to an object, became the focus of poetic experience and endeavor. According to the early formalists, poetic language was characterized by a unique organization of phonic matter. Other formal principles of language were submitted to a phonically based interpretation. Thus, O. Brik analyzed syntactic parallelism as a sound repetition (Pomorska, 1968:28).

The exclusion of the meaning level as in so-called *zaumnyj* ("transmental," "transrational," "supraconscious," etc.) poetry could not be consistently maintained. In the formation of sound matter, these poets resorted to morphological patterns, if not from their own language, then from foreign languages. Turkic languages were especially appealing since their "difficult forms" were useful for one goal in particular of the futurists: the disautomatization of sound perception. Furthermore, "supraconscious" poetry soon emerged not as poetry without meaning, but as a poetry capable of evoking both new meanings and meanings torn out of their familiar context. An "objectless" poetry became an "object-*estranged*" poetry (ibid., 109, 122).

In Jakobson's early studies on poetry, the original exclusion of the thematic level from poetry by the futurists appears in the revised form of the exclusion of reference to physical things (1921a:92) and of the truth function of utterances. The poet is not interested in the truth content of his utterances. Therefore, he cannot be held responsible for the ideas he presents.

To incriminate the poet with ideas and emotions is as absurd as the behavior of the medieval audiences that beat the actor who played Judas and just as foolish as blaming Pushkin for the death of Lensky. (1921a:40)

The poet as such is interested only in the extrication and creative utilization of the processes and regularity constitutive of language, whereby meanings function as principles of form or—to use the terminology preferred by Jakobson—as principles of structure quite as much as the other elements of language. The structural makeup of a poem involves its semantic and grammatical nature as well as its phonological and metrical nature.

> "Composition" [of the poem] here means not only the strictly external signs, the [so-called] formal expression, but also the semantics of that formal expression. I do not like to use the terms "contents" and "form." The contents are part of the structure of the poem. The structure includes both the *signifiant* and the *signifié* of the verbal signs and their composition. There is a relation between the form and the contents. The contents are part of the form, just as the form is part of the contents. Anton Marty, the Swiss friend of Husserl, has published a remarkable study [1879] about this subject. (1973b:8f., 23, 60)

Homo- and heteromorphisms play a decisive role in making the various levels of language conscious (1966c). Syntactic parallelism clashes with semantic opposition: "The clever one boasts of his golden stock,/The stupid one boasts of his young wife" (1961b:600). The repetition of synonymous expressions brings out in two different expressions a meaning that remains identical: "He is naked and bare" (1921a:112). The play on homonyms is also based on incongruity between meaning and expression: "The *kosa* ['braid' or 'scythe'] sometimes adorns the head, hanging down to the shoulders; sometimes cuts the grass" (ibid.). In all three cases the difference in sameness is the vehicle for making the interrelated levels of language conscious.

An oxymoron is characterized by the emancipation of meaning from its referent. Historical and physical facts are not important. Only a play on linguistic elements that have become autonomous is intended, in this case on meanings and systems of meanings:

> "... when they cut off his [the saint's] head at last, he got up, picked up the head, and politely kissed it." [Dostoevskij] . In this case a human being is simply a traditional semantic unit which retains all of its attributes; in other words the semantic unit has become fixed. (1921a:50)

An extremely effective means of making linguistic forms visible is deformation. This, too, exists not only on the sound level but also on the meaning level. Familiar in colloquial speech is the substitution of an initial consonant to make an inner connection of meanings visible (e.g., Russian *devjat'* 'nine' derived from *desjat'* 'ten'). Frequently the substitution appears as a lapsus. Xlebnikov uses it as a poetic device, and an effective one at that.

> The word in question thus gains as it were a new sound character. Its meaning wavers, and the word is apprehended as an acquaintance with a suddenly unfamiliar face, or as a stranger in whom we are able to see something familiar. (1921a:106)

Semantic estrangement is achieved by the use of unusual words, archaisms, barbarisms, provincialisms, and neologisms (1921a:66, 84ff.). Conversely, the very use of ordinary expressions and an ordinary style for a matter which we have become accustomed to clothing in exceptional, "exalted," or archaic speech reveals it in a new or perhaps forgotten semantic context.

The hermeneutic restriction of the interpretation of poems to their *sens vécu* represents a grave mutilation of poetic texts. There is also a *forme vécue* that is no less a psychological reality than the meaning of linguistic signs (see 1973a:502). In poetry, connections between sounds act as inductors of sense relations (paronomasia: Lat. *nomen est omen* 'name–fame'). Rhyme is a sound phenomenon with a semantic function (see 1960b:368f.).

> In poetry, any conspicuous similarity in sound is evaluated in respect to similarity and/or dissimilarity in meaning. (ibid., 372)

> Words similar in sound are drawn together in meaning. (ibid., 371)

One point of departure in hermeneutic interpretation is the ambiguity of poetic texts. Ambiguity is viewed as an ultimate fact, or rather as a datum in the strict sense of the word, as a gift of grace, which can be elucidated only to a very limited extent. Structuralism, on the other hand, views ambiguity as the result of a consciously or unconsciously applied device. It can in principle be explained. One of the simplest vehicles of ambiguity is the evocation of a second meaning on the basis of phonological, metrical, or syntactic equivalence, as in the following Russian wedding song:

> A fierce horse was coming at gallop to the court,
> A brave fellow was going to the porch,
> Vasilij was walking to the manor.

The "fierce horse" is a possession of the bridegroom and becomes his image through metrical and syntactic parallels with him. A metaphorical relation is superimposed upon a metonymical one (1960b:369f.).

The paper "Linguistics and Poetics" (1960b) delineates in concentrated form Jakobson's theory of poetry as it has evolved in his researches over the last forty years. Jakobson decidedly rejects the restriction of poetry to the sound level as "phonetic isolationism." For his point of view he choses Valery's formula, "hesitation between the sound and the sense" (1960b:367). He also disclaims his own Moscow and Prague thesis (1921a:92; 1934:414), according to which the objective reference of language is absent in poetry. "The supremacy of poetic function over referential function does not obliterate the reference but makes it ambiguous" (1960b:371). The essence of poetry, "poeticity," is no longer to be sought in the additional appearance of a linguistic element or, conversely, in the elimination of one. What characterizes poetry is the conscious play with autonomy and interdependence of the various levels and factors of language. This is achieved by the rigorous structuring of levels and the play on their interaction, their overlapping, and their reciprocal complement and contrast (see 1962d).

> A missionary blamed his African flock for walking undressed. "And what about yourself?" they pointed to his visage, "are not you, too, somewhere naked?" "Well, but that is my face." "Yet in us," retorted the natives, "everywhere it is face." So in poetry any verbal element is converted into a figure of poetic speech. (1960b:377)

2.3.2.4. *Meaning and reference.* Repudiation of the exclusion of the objective reference as the cardinal characteristic of poetry coincides with a new concept of the reference of language, which Jakobson touches upon in the above-mentioned paper (1960b:353) and develops in more detail in recent lectures (1973b:52ff.).

The current discussion on the distinction between meaning and reference dates back to Frege (1892). It is based on the observation that two expressions may have different meanings but the same object, or the same meaning and different objects. Frege gives the following example for the first case: "morning star" and "evening star" are two expressions with a different meaning but the same object, the planet Venus. Husserl gives the following example for the second case: when we say "Bucephalus is a horse" at one time and "that cart horse is a nag" at another, then the meaning of the expression "a horse" remains constant in the transition from one sentence to the other, but its reference has changed.

Jakobson originally concurred with this distinction, set forth in Husserl's *Logical Investigations* (1913:286ff.; Jakobson, 1936b:SW II 34; 1941:SW I 354), but has, in recent publications (1973b:52; 1975d), raised the objection that "morning star" and "evening star" do not, indeed, have the same referent. They refer to two different phases of the appearance of the planet Venus. We cannot substitute the expression "morning star" for "evening star" in every situation.* Every object always appears in a situation, in a network of relations that is defined temporally, spatially, or by its content and that must be taken into account in determination of the referent. We cannot designate an object without, at the same time, introducing it into a situation or a context. If I make an appointment at "5:45," then I use a retrospective designative system; if at "a quarter to six," then a prospective one, which is, in addition, less precise than the first. The second system of relations allows a certain temporal leeway. "5:45" means exactly 5:45. Every denotation is at the same time a connotation.

We can extend Jakobson's observations by saying that there is no absolute "thing in itself," no x, which can be completely detached from its modes of givenness. If we wish to explain the reference of expressions such as "morning star" and "evening star," we have no choice but to recur to a further mode of givenness or a description of the meant, such as "the star that the Romans called Venus" or "the second-closest planet to the sun." The network of relations is different every time. The problem of truth is not the correspondence between a meaning and a referent, but rather the compatibility between two meanings, two modes of givenness, or two contextual determinations.

The question of truth or existence, as Jakobson (1973b:52f.) sees it, can only be raised in relation to a context. Every indefinite existential utterance—"Ambrosia exists," "Quarks exist"—is an elliptical utterance requiring completion by an indication of which system of meanings it is operative in. Ambrosia exists in the framework of Greek mythology. And within this framework, not only meaningful but also true and untrue statements can be made about ambrosia. The gods eat ambrosia, they don't drink it. Quarks, i.e., the hypothetical subparticles into which the currently

*Frege (1892:92f.) treats irreplaceability only in linguistic contexts in which expressions are used "obliquely," i.e., when not the object but the meaning itself is intended.

known subatomic particles are said to be further divisible, exist in the framework of a specific new theory of physics. *Quark* as a kind of cottage cheese exists in the framework of sensorily perceivable things.

There is no matter without form. But there is also no form without a material determination. Every system of relations in space and time has a point of departure and a criterion, both of which are defined by content—the birth of Christ, Greenwich, the rotation of the earth around the sun, a foot, etc. The delimitation of invariant abstract structures is only one goal of research. The other goal is to determine which kinds of concrete objects allow the representation of a given abstract structure.

2.4. *Taxonomy and teleonomy*

2.4.1. *Taxonomy—an indictment?* The names of trends in the sciences and arts often have a capricious career. There are titles that the initiators of a movement have themselves suggested, only to use them later with many reservations and limitations. Too many colleagues who have chosen to take only part of the same path and too many followers who have only understood half of what it is all about issue their studies under the same successful heading. "Structuralism," brought forward by Jakobson in 1929, is such a title.

Other titles stem not from the advocates of a movement, but from its critics. And not infrequently, a title conceived as an indictment by the opponent, subsequently takes a positive turn and is adopted by representatives of the criticized movement as an illuminating designation, one that has opened up unexpected vistas. A case in point is "formalism," coined by opponents of the program and studies of the linguists and literary scholars in Moscow and Petersburg. The rise of gestalt psychology supplied the Moscow and Petersburg avant-garde with the opportunity to give this epithet a positive turn. Many languages render the German *Gestaltpsychologie* with "psychology of form." And indeed, the Russian formalists as well as gestalt psychologists did not pursue forms and formulas stripped of content, but rather the creative principles of gestalt constitutive of particular phenomena.

For over ten years, a designation intended as an indictment has been imposed on structural linguistics as well. As a collective term for the phonology developed by the most varied representatives of a structural method, Chomsky (1964:75) coined the term *taxonomic phonemics.* Earlier in the same work (11), he had already juxtaposed a taxonomic and a transformational model of grammar. As a result, *taxonomic* fast became a pejorative attribute, applied to the entire field of structural linguistics regardless of the divergencies of the different schools.

It is not always clear in Chomsky's writings to what extent he wishes to implicate Jakobson and his Prague colleagues in the criticism. At the beginning of the publication where he formulates his criticism of taxonomy for the first time, he thanks his teachers at the University of Pennsylvania and at Harvard, Zellig Harris and Roman Jakobson. He states that his account of linguistic structure "in part incorporates and in part developed in response to many stimulating ideas" of these two. In the text which then follows, as in his other discussions of structuralism, one finds passages in which Jakobson is expressly excluded from the criticism and others where he and Trubetzkoy are included by name. But even these passages do not provide a clear indication of the extent of the criticism. Embedded among disparaging and wholesale value judgments are informative delineations of the achievements and fields of application of structural linguistics.

> The structure of a phonological system is of very little interest as a formal object; there is nothing of significance to be said, from a formal point of view, about a set of forty-odd elements cross-classified in terms of eight or ten features. The significance of structuralist phonology, as developed by Troubetzkoy, Jakobson, and others, lies not in the formal properties of phonemic systems but in the fact that a fairly small number of features that

can be specified in absolute, language-independent terms appear to provide the basis for the organization of all phonological systems. The achievement of structuralist phonology was to show that the phonological rules of a great variety of languages apply to classes of elements that can be simply characterized in terms of these features; that historical change affects such classes in a uniform way; and that the organization of features plays a basic role in the use and acquisition of language. . . . But if we abstract away from the specific universal set of features and the rule systems in which they function, little of any significance remains. (Chomsky, 1972a:74f.)

Jakobson himself occasionally uses the term taxonomy (1958b:SW I 524; 1962e:SW II 284) and also makes reference to research into biological systems, the original home of this term. (It occurs more frequently in Lévi-Strauss [1962].) These references throw light on the role of taxonomy within the various branches of linguistics. In recent publications, Jakobson avoids the term in protest to the simplifying interpretations to which structuralism has been subjected under this heading. It seems to us that this title can also be viewed in a positive light. To illuminate this possibility, we commence with a synopsis of taxonomic principles and procedures, as criticized by Chomsky, on the one hand, and understood by Jakobson, on the other.

2.4.2. *Taxonomic principles.*

2.4.2.1. *Segmentation and classification.* Chomsky (1964:11, 75) cites segmentation and classification as the fundamental procedures of taxonomic linguistics. A given corpus—texts, in the case of language—is subdivided into discrete units. The problem of segmentation of the corpus and classification of its elements lies in identification of the variants. Which data can be taken as instances of the same unit? In phonology, three criteria are usually named for the identification of a phoneme: phonetic resemblance, complementary distribution, and commutability.

For Jakobson (1962a:SW I 640), *phonetic resemblance*

is a vague and misleading criterion. It does not take into account the specifically linguistic form and function of phonemes or their distinctive features, which reside in their relational nature and meaning-differentiation. Phonological invariants cannot be measured absolutely. The criterion of metric resemblance is replaced by that of relational equivalence. Thus, in the Bulgarian vowel system with the three pairs /e/ – /i/, /o/ – /u/, /a/ – /ə/, the physico-motor kinship between the /ə/ of the last pair and the /e/ and /o/ of the other two pairs is not decisive, but rather the opposition of relatively compact and relatively diffuse, which underlies all three pairs. This oppositional relation, applicable as a gestalt quality to the different, varying data, determines the identification of a phoneme, and not the datum itself measured in isolation. Gestalt qualities are not affected by modifications of the concrete data upon which they are based.

According to the criterion of *complementary distribution,* two or more sounds represent one and the same phoneme when they are similar but mutually exclusive in a certain phonetic environment. A distribution of this kind is demonstrated by the German [ç] and [x]. After /i/ only a [ç] (*ich*) can occur, after /a/ only a [x] (*ach*). [ç] and [x] are therefore considered contextual variants of the same phoneme /x/.

According to Jakobson (1951:SW I 436), complementary distribution cannot act as an absolute criterion intralingually. In Danish the pretonic *d* and posttonic *d* are similar and mutually exclusive in the same position. However, they function indisputably as two distinct phonemes. Jakobson shows that interlingually the criterion of complementary distribution proves to be exceedingly fruitful in setting up a phonological typology of languages. Through its application, it becomes possible to reduce what at first sight seems a great diversity of distinctive features to a small number. The following law results.

If two or more allegedly different features never co-occur in a language, and if they, furthermore, yield a common property distinguishing them from all other features, then they are to be interpreted as different implementations of one and the same feature, each occurring to the exclusion of the others and, consequently, presenting a particular case of complementary distribution. (1956a:SW I 483)

Thus, the opposition implosive/explosive, found in some African languages, need not be added to the inventory of distinctive features; it has been established (1962a:SW I 654) that, in languages displaying this opposition, either the opposition glottalized/nonglottalized is absent, or the voiced glottalized stops appear in free variation with voiced implosives, or, finally, the opposition glottalized/nonglottalized is represented by voiceless and the opposition implosive/ explosive by voiced stops. Each of these isomorphic pairs displays the same relation of a reduced and a nonreduced portion of air as well as basically the same acoustic differences.

Commutability is a functional criterion. If a phonic variation entails a semantic variation, then the two mutually exchanged phonic units are considered two distinct phonemes. Should no change of meaning take place, then they are two variants of the same phoneme. The commutation test shows, for example, that *p* and *b* represent two variants of one phoneme in Finnish, but two autonomous phonemes in English. If *b* takes the place of the *p* in *pay*, another word results. *Bay* differs in meaning from *pay*.

The limitations of the commutation test are exhibited in homonyms and synonyms. Chomsky (1957a:94ff.) cites examples such as *bank* and /ekɨnamiks/ vs. /iykɨnamiks/ (*economics*). The phonological structure of *bank* does not illuminate its ambiguity ("bank of a river," "savings bank"); the application of the commutation test to the second example would lead an investigator not familiar with English to the fallacious conclusion that *e* and *iy* are two variants of the same phoneme. The fact that commutability is not an absolute criterion does not, however, for Jakobson

(1962a:SW I 656ff.) interfere with its usefulness and indispensability. The virtual semantic relevance of distinctive features is usually not fully utilized in speech. Language is a highly redundant means of communication. Isolated phonemes are not the only means of differentiating meaning. The context, both verbal and nonverbal (the situation), can also indicate whether the bank of a river or a savings bank is meant. Furthermore, the presence of exceptions is a "weakness" shared by the semantically based definition of a phonological entity with the majority of functional definitions. An end can in principle be achieved by various means. With regard to synonymous expressions, it must also be mentioned that the variants easily acquire a stylistic value.

2.4.2.2. *Linearity and invariance.* Chomsky (1964:78) lists four conditions assumed by taxonomic phonology for phonological entities: linearity, invariance, biuniqueness, and local determinacy. Before discussing these conditions, we shall present Jakobson's more general definitions of the terms *linearity* and *invariance,* which differ from Chomsky's usage.

In his *Cours* (1916:70), Saussure lists linearity as the second fundamental characteristic of linguistic signs, following that of arbitrariness. In contradistinction to visual signs, which can unfold along several dimensions simultaneously, auditive signs have, according to Saussure, only the one dimension of time at their disposal. One element follows another. "It is impossible to pronounce two sounds at the same time" (Bally, quoted by Jakobson, 1939a:SW I 305). Jakobson finds the absolute priority of the temporal axis in Saussure untenable. It obstructs the progress of phonological research, i.e., the exploration and recognition of the differential elements upon which phonemes build simultaneously. Saussure's student, Bally, speaks of a *cumul de signifiés* ("accumulation of *signata*") on the level of the *signatum;* correspondingly, one could, according to Jakobson, speak of a *cumul de signifiants* ("accumulation of *signantia*") on the level of the *signans.*

The ending of the Latin verb *amo* 'I love' signals several meanings at once: the first person in contrast to *amas* 'you love', the singular in contrast to *amamus* 'we love', the present in contrast to *amabam* 'I loved', and so on. A parallel accumulation of values is shown on the level of the *signantia.* The English phoneme /b/ in *buy* is oral (nonnasal) in contrast to the nasal /m/ in *my*, discontinuant in contrast to the continuant /v/ in *vie,* lax in contrast to the tense /p/ in *pie,* grave in contrast to the acute /d/ in *die*, both grave and lax in contrast to the acute and tense /s/ in *sigh*, and so on.

Saussure's principle of linearity cannot be sustained. Besides the concept of sound sequence, Jakobson, as early as 1932, added to the definition of the phoneme the formula "a set of ... concurrent sound properties," which he later replaced by the formula "a bundle of distinctive features," following Bloomfield's (1933:79) terminology. Accordingly, questions of distribution and context are directed not only at preceding and succeeding but at simultaneous factors as well. Music, too, not only displays combinations on the axis of succession (sequence) but also "complications" on the axis of simultaneity (chords) (1932c:SW I 231; 1949a:SW I 420; 1962a:SW I 636).

Ever since mathematics in the years around 1870 turned toward systematic study of the interplay of *invariance* and *variation,* these concepts have played an increasingly significant role in the methodological discussion of all sciences. Their cardinal position is to be explained by the aim of every science to extract the simplest and most generally valid findings possible. The most popular example is Newton's law of gravity. Newton succeeded in demonstrating that the seemingly disparate behavior of earthly and heavenly bodies—apples fall to earth vertically, planets move in orbit around the sun—can be explained by the same law. Common to both, the invariance in the variance, is the fact that they are masses subject to the law of gravity. Whenever a structure or a law is discovered, the question of the extent and conditions of its application immediately arises. Across which variations or transformations does the structure retain its invariance?

This approach is systematically applied by structuralism

to linguistics and the science of literature. But, besides the general scientific intention, the search for invariants in linguistics is propelled by a specifically linguistic motivation as well. The development of invariants is founded on the communicative function of language. Intersubjective communication rests on the use of uniform means. It implies intralingual invariants and, furthermore, leads to the emergence of interlingual common ground. The very fact that interlingual translations are possible and necessary indicates the existence of interlingual invariants, known as universals.

> The primary tendency of communication is its diffusion, so that communication becomes still more generalized. One of the most harmful scientific isolationisms has been intralingual isolationism. Because, in point of fact, there is no "iron curtain" between languages. Whether two peoples are at peace or at war, cold or hot, linguistic interrelations continue, since in the latter case it is necessary at times to spy, at times to discuss and negotiate. When interlingual relation exists, then there occurs perpetual accommodation, a tendency to find a common code. . . . (1953d:292)

In phonetics, vowels and consonants were long considered two quite disparate groups with no common denominator. Jakobson succeeded in bridging the gap. On the level of articulation, this unification was prepared by the replacement of the crude, traditional division of consonants according to their place of articulation (labial, dental, guttural, etc.) with an arrangement based on truly relevant factors—the size and shape of the resonance cavity and the relationship between the flow of air and its obstruction. Jakobson demonstrated that the two oppositional pairs compact/diffuse and grave/acute are invariant structures common to vowels and consonants. He found authoritative precursors to his endeavors among the ancient Indian grammarians, who had already established a connection between the k-series and a and the p/t-series and u/i.

The spectrographic diagram (see Figure 5) of labial and dental consonants in French clearly illustrates the invariance of the distinctive features, which appear in varying combination with other features.* The three horizontal bands represent the acoustic formants (concentration of acoustic energy). The downward movement of the highest formant of the labials uniformly distinguishes them from the dentals, in which the upward movement of the same formant is typical or invariant.

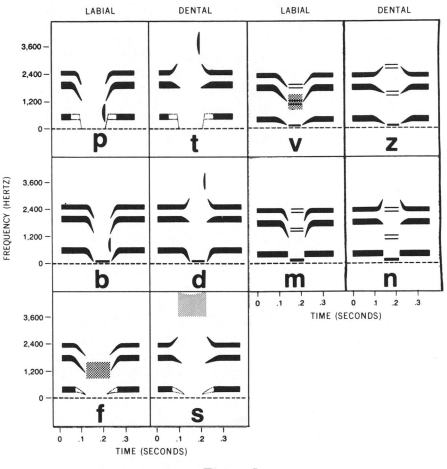

Figure 5

*The diagram, a slightly simplified version of that in 1972a:74, stems from the phonetician Pierre Delattre (1968:199), who worked with Jakobson on the acoustic analysis of distinctive features.

Refuting the widespread empiricist notion that all meanings are bound to the situation, Jakobson defends the existence of invariants in semantics as well. Exclusively contextual meanings are characteristic only of one special case of linguistic reality, a certain type of aphasia (similarity disorder). Two outstanding linguistic achievements in particular are based on the existence of invariant semantic values: the ability to introduce words into new contexts and the ability to translate. We cannot use or understand a word in a new context unless we are already familiar with certain components of the context, i.e., unless these components possess an invariant semantic value (1953a:SW II 225). In translation as well, we orient ourselves on the basis of the invariant values of the signs. The term *universals* has come to designate interlingual invariants. This term from traditional linguistics (see the Port-Royal *Grammaire générale et raisonnée*), proscribed by empirical schools of thought, has once again become a cardinal concept of the new linguistics, in part thanks to Jakobson's influence (Greenberg, 1963).* Chomsky (1965:25ff.) makes a distinction between formal and substantive universals. Substantive universals are the elements common to all languages. In illustration, Chomsky cites Jakobson's theory of distinctive features, which states that the smallest phonological elements in each language are taken from a universal stock of elements. Formal universals refer to the structures and organization of linguistic rules.

In Jakobson, a different grouping dominates. He insists especially on two categories of universals, on relational invariants and on rules of implication (1963a:SW II 581f.). Toward universals defined in absolute terms, he expresses

---

*Martinet in an interview with Parret (1974:227): "It is not fortuitous that linguistic *universals* were introduced by Jakobson. The Aginskys' paper [1948], which was the first to mention linguistic universals, had been ordered by Jakobson. It took some time for the seed to bear fruit, but, ever since, what has been produced is in the same vein. From the moment that everybody began to speak about *universals* I saw the shadow of Jakobson. They all yielded: even Hockett contributed to Greenberg's book [1963]. Greenberg himself, who often opposed Jakobson when he and I were co-editors of *Word*, also swallowed the bait."

great scepticism. Relational invariants are exemplified in phonology by the oppositions compact/diffuse and acute/grave. Universal relations in grammar are exemplified by the difference between the noun class and verb class and between their correlated but not simply congruent functions of subject and predicate.

Jakobson's most original contribution to the theory of universals lies in the extrication of universal rules of implication. These concern the compatibility and incompatibility of relational features. The laws of implication were first uncovered in phonology and later also on the levels of morphology and syntax.

> Thus in phonemics the combinability of distinctive features into bundles or sequences is restricted and determined by a considerable number of universal implicational rules. For instance, the concurrence of nasality with the vocalic feature implies its concurrence with the consonantal feature. A compact nasal consonant (/ɲ/ or /ŋ/) implies the presence of two diffuse consonants, one acute (/n/) and the other grave (/m/). (1963a:SW II 582)

Jakobson models his formulation of the rules of implication, as already mentioned, on Husserl's doctrine of foundedness. His application of the rules to the problem of invariants and universals, however, goes beyond Husserl and the entire classical conception of the determination of essences. A first extension arose out of the basically relational determination of the elements of a class (2.3.2.2. above). The second extension lies in the observation that the occurrence of universal features is subject to laws of condition. The classical doctrine of essences embraces only absolute, necessarily actualized invariants. Invariants of a thing include, for instance, that it is extended in three dimensions, displays a real-causal dependence of its features on its environment (a piece of iron expands with rising temperature), and can only be perceived in perspective, etc. If one of these eidetic determinations is absent, then we are no longer confronted with a thing but with, perhaps, a phantom. Jakobson does not treat the features of a single element, but those of a system of elements. The system is submitted to a typological examination. It is compared with other systems. In phonology certain features were found to appear in all systems, others only in some systems. Of significance here is the discovery that features are not randomly present or absent. The presence or absence of a feature is bound to the presence or absence of other features. This means that substantive elements are not universal in the absolute sense, but the laws of implication are. Substantive elements are for the most part only potentially universal. Hence, as an example of a universal law, the statement can be presented that a language never utilizes all phonological oppositions.

Jakobson's conception lies between Husserl's doctrine of essences and Wittgenstein's (1968: §§ 66f.) thesis of "family resemblances." According to Wittgenstein's thesis, the elements of a class, like the members of a family, are characterized by various features, none of which is, however, to be found in all the elements without exception. Given is a complex network of resemblances in which only groups of elements, never the entire class of combined elements, participate. Jakobson diverges from Wittgenstein as to the nonarbitrariness, the rigorously ordered presence and absence, of features. Besides the general laws of implication, which define the stratification of a system, there are also laws of compensation. The more complex an entity, the less open it is to further fission. Due to the complex character of the plural as opposed to the simple singular, it is understandable that differentiation according to gender is a less frequent occurrence in the plural than in the singular (cf. the French articles *les* vs. *le, la*).

In addition to proper universals, there are *near-universals*. Their discovery does not betoken that universals can only be verified statistically. They are an indication of a fundamental tendency or preference of the language system. Jakobson plainly distinguishes between an analytical and a purely statistical examination of universals. "In the search for the general meaning of a form, the statistical criterion is inapplicable—usual meaning and general meaning are not synonymous" (1932b:SW II 9). The cardinal task in the exploration of universals consists in deducing them "from as small a number of general principles as possible" (Greenberg, cited by Jakobson, 1963a:SW II 585) and in elucidating their exceptions on the basis of competing principles. With its theory of invariants and universals, Jakobson's structuralism also counters a distinction propagated in neo-Kantian and hermeneutic circles, the distinction between *nomothetic* natural sciences, which "set up laws" for the uniform, recurring events of nature, and *ideographic* humanities, whose alleged cardinal concern are the basically "unique" phenomena of culture, which are not subject to general laws, but can only be described in terms of their respective "idiosyncrasy." It is worthy of note that nowhere in this historical distinction is there talk of linguistics. For Jakobson, linguistics, poetics, and the theory of literature are nomothetic sciences. The studies on the history of linguistics in the second volume of *Selected Writings* are entitled "Toward a Nomothetic Science of Language." The Russian formalists disclaimed the traditional histories of art and literature, which, in Jakobson's words, were no science, but causerie:

> [They] obeyed all the laws of causerie, skipping blithely from topic to topic, from lyrical effusions on the elegance of forms to anecdotes from the artist's life, from psychological truisms to questions concerning philosophical significance and social environment. . . . In causerie we are slipshod with our terminology. (1921b:38)

The Russian formalists responded by launching a rigorously scientific approach to the study of literature:

> The subject of literary scholarship is not literature but literariness (*literaturnost*), that is, that which makes of a given work a work of literature. (1921a:30)

Similarly, the object of poetics, "poeticity," is defined as that which distinguishes a poetic text from other linguistic texts (1934:413). The somewhat cumbersome word formations, "literariness" and "poeticity," again recall Husserl's theory of eidetic abstraction, which was developed primarily in terms of "thingness" as that which makes a thing (of perception) a thing. Husserl, too, had moved away from Dilthey's negation of "pure universals" in the sphere of the humanities.

We now return to Chomsky's criticism of phonological taxonomy, which he presents under the headings of linearity, invariance, biuniqueness, and local determinacy. Chomsky makes very narrow use of the first two terms in comparison to what has been stated above. Chomsky's linearity condition is a designation for the assumption that each occurrence of a phoneme on the phonemic level is represented by a unique sequence of (one or more) consecutive phones on the phonetic level. If, on the phonemic level, *A* precedes *B,* then on the phonetic level the sequence of sounds associated with *A* also precedes that associated with *B.* The invariance condition asserts that every phoneme has associated with it a certain set of defining features and that, in its phonetic representation as well, each occurrence of a phoneme appears with its corresponding set of features. In illustration of a violation of these two correlated conditions, Chomsky (1964:82) cites the words *writer* and *rider.* They differ phonemically in their fourth segments (tense *t* / lax *d*) and phonetically in their second segments (short *a* / long *a*).

	phonemic	*phonetic*
writer	rayt#ɨr	rayDɨr
rider	rayd#ɨr	ra˙yDɨr

Jakobson's analysis (1968:SW I 713) of this example is most instructive with regard to the linguistic model upon which his analyses are based. For variations of this kind in surface structure, he does not, like Chomsky, recur to a posited, abstract underlying structure, transformable via equally abstract rules into completely different surface structures, but rather to other, affiliated, i.e., genetically and phenomenologically correlated, surface structures. Thus, in the above example, he distinguishes between the elliptical code of slovenly speech and the explicit, optimal code of careful speech. The more explicit the code, the stronger is the tendency to discriminate the tenseness and laxness of the intervocalic phones *t* and *d*. The most stable cue for the distinction between tense and lax phonemes is the greater duration of the former. The relative length of the middle consonant in *writer* implies a shortening of the preceding syllabic. In the subcode of hasty speech, the difference in the quantitative relation between vowel and consonant can chiefly or only be signalized by the varying duration of the preceding vowel. In Jakobson's opinion, Chomsky's criticism strikes at misguided phonological analyses in which the phoneme is still treated as an indivisible, ultimate entity. It loses its vigor as soon as it is applied to an analysis based on relational features, and a fundamental distinction is made between the explicit code, upon which Jakobson's analysis of features is grounded, and its elliptical variants.

2.4.2.3. *Autonomy vs. interrelation of linguistic levels.* In the third and fourth conditions of taxonomic phonemics as well, more is involved than mere technical detail. Here the important question arises of the interrelation of the manifold levels of language.

The third condition asserts that each sequence of sound realizations corresponds to a unique sequence of phonemes and vice versa. Again, for Jakobson, this condition of biuniqueness is not tenable unless one accounts for the relational structure of the phonological invariants which are not affected by the diverse contextual variations. The thesis that this condition is not applicable to a purely metrical determination of sounds is one of the oldest themes of Jakobson's phonology (see 1956a:SW I 473, quoted above 1.4.3.). According to the fourth condition, local determinacy, only the immediate phonic environment of a sequence of sounds is taken into consideration in the determination of its corresponding phonemic structure. Chomsky

(1964:101ff.) sees the third and fourth conditions as motivated by the assumption of a rigid separation of the different levels of language, an assumption upon which various advocates of a taxonomic phonemics build their conception of the linguist's investigation of language and the child's acquisition of it. Chomsky, on the other hand, following Halle, defends a relative autonomy or, as he puts it, a "non-autonomy of phonology" (not to be confused with "inseparability"). Certain—but not all—phonetic processes are dependent upon syntactic and morphological structure, so that the study of phonology cannot proceed in complete independence of higher structural levels. This thesis recalls Jakobson's methodological basis for interdisciplinary research, which he also declares valid for the relation of intralinguistic disciplines.

> Two methodological principles may further the prospective inquiry into speech perception. They could be labeled AUTONOMY and INTEGRATION. Each level of language from its ultimate discrete components of the totality of discourse and each level of speech production and perception must be treated with respect both to intrinsic, autonomous laws and to the constant interaction of diverse levels as well as to the integral structure of the verbal code and messages (alias LANGUAGE and SPEECH) in their permanent interplay. The necessary tie between these two fundamental principles warns the investigator against two traditional blunders. These are, on the one hand, ISOLATIONISM, which deliberately disregards the interconnections of the parts and their solidarity with the whole, and on the other hand, HETERONOMY (or, metaphorically, COLONIALISM), which forcibly subjects one level to another's rules and denies the former's own patterning as well as its self-generating development. (1968:SW I 716)

In a report for the Sixth International Congress of Linguists in Paris, Jakobson (1949b:SW II 103ff.) explicitly and in detail repudiated the thesis, proscribed by Chomsky, of the absolute separation of structural levels. Building on the definition of the phoneme as a meaning-differentiating entity, he discusses the dependence of the phonological pattern of an utterance on grammatical entities. "The combinations of phonemes are different at the beginning, within, and at the end of a word" (ibid., 106). Certain phonological oppositions are to be found exclusively in certain grammatical classes of formal units. Of the twenty-three consonants in Czech, only eight appear in productive inflections. In certain Turkic languages, the articulatory oppositions back/front have a distinctive function only in the stem and not in the suffixes. "In short, an attempt to confine oneself to a simple inventory of the distinctive features and of their simultaneous and successive configurations without any grammatical specification of their use would be an artificial projection of different layers upon one plane" (ibid., 109).

From the familiar observation that linguistic utterances remain understandable even with severe distortion, Chomsky (1964:99f.) arrives at the extreme conclusion that the pregivenness of grammatical structures can completely replace phonetic clues. Jakobson resists this generalization. Citing perceptual analyses of linguistic patterns in Russian, Jakobson (1968:SW I 706f.), well aware of how embedded phonemes are in a syntactic and semantic environment, defends the inevitable necessity of starting from a purely phonological base in the decoding of linguistic utterances.

In the 1949 report quoted above, Jakobson further emphasizes the "more than labile" limit between phonology proper and morphonology. Jakobson acclaims the so-called generative phonology of Halle and Chomsky for having submitted the field of morphonology, which the Prague phonologists had only begun to explore, to systematic examination. Mor[pho]phonology treats of the morphological employ of phonological differences. The study of phonological alternations within morphemes and classes of morphemes (e.g., the alternation of $e - a - i$ in different forms of German verbs: *ich gebe — ich gab — er gibt*) led to a new conception of the paradigmatic classes of phonemes; static arrangements became dynamic systems of structured convergencies and divergencies. However, while generative phonology views the morphoneme as an "abstract" entity underlying various concrete sound realizations (e.g., the morphological segment /ī/ underlies the phonetic segments [ay] and [i] in *divine* and *divinity*), the Prague linguists defined the morphoneme as a "complex" entity (*idée complexe,* CLP, 1931b:322). The phonic alternants ([ay] and [i] in the above illustration) "are experienced as two phonic forms of one and the same morpheme, which lives in the linguistic conscious in two phonic forms at the same time" (Trubetzkoy, 1929:85).

The conception of the Prague theorists is more phenomenological than that of generative grammar and phonology. It adheres to the intuitive givenness of linguistic facts in the linguistic conscious and does not prematurely recur to abstract entities (see Derwing, 1973:91ff.) as substrates of phenomenological data, for which a neurological reality is then postulated since they cannot be found by introspection. It states that various linguistic data, which need not be simultaneously actualized, refer to each other intentionally (in colloquial speech, "the one recalls the other") and are associatively bound to each other.

2.4.2.4. *Formation vs. transformation.* A more phenomenological treatment of linguistic data is also displayed in Jakobson's consideration of the problematic of transformation in syntax, which, due to Chomsky, has become a cardinal concern of linguistic research. For a full and unambiguous understanding of certain linguistic utterances, an analysis of the successive categories on the syntagmatic axis does not suffice. Only a reformulation on the paradigmatic axis reveals a potential ambiguity. According to one of Chomsky's many examples, "John kept the car in the garage" is ambiguous (although only in written form or in elliptical, slovenly pronunciation), as shown by the two passive renditions of the sentence: "The car was kept in the garage by John" and "The car in the garage was kept by John."

We have mentioned that Jakobson sees the principal merit of generative phonology in the elaboration of the morphonological problematic. He sees the principal merit of generative transformational grammar in its having surmounted the Saussurian thesis that "every syntactical fact belongs to the syntagmatic class" (1916:137). "So-called transformational grammar may be viewed as an auspicious extension of a paradigmatic analysis to the sphere of syntax" (1974e:21). Both disciplines reject another Saussurian assumption, which Jakobson had already contested in his morphological studies of the thirties, namely, the assumption (1916:126) that the units on the paradigmatic axis manifest an indeterminate order (1958b:SW I 524f.). In the conception of the paradigmatic hierarchy, however, Jakobson and Chomsky part ways.

As he does so many linguistic questions, Jakobson approaches the topic of transformation from the side of poetry. A cardinal term of Russian formalism, connected with the principle of estrangement, was deformation, the conscious phonic, morphological, syntactic, and semantic reshaping of linguistic patterns (1921a:90). The antigrammatical constructions of futuristic poets, abhorred by conservative critics as destructive, cleared the path for the discovery of the basically no less astonishing linguistic constructions underlying the generally accepted poetic and rhetorical tropes and figures. The best known is the personification of properties and actions—linguistically speaking, the nominalization of adjectives and verbs.

> When in the finale of Majakovskij's poem *Xoroso* we read—"*i žízn'/xorošá,//i žít'/xorošó//*" (literally "both life is good, and it is good to live")—one will hardly look for a cognitive difference between these two coordinate clauses, but in poetic mythology the linguistic fiction of the substantivized and hence hypostatized process grows into a metonymic image of life as such, taken by itself and substituted for the living people, *abstractum pro concreto*. . . . (1961b:599)

In the transition from formalism to structuralism, the term *transformation* replaced *deformation* (Pomorska, 1968:40). Their familiarity with poetry rescued the propo-

nents of Prague structuralism from the antisemantic fallacies
of early transformational grammar. In such sentences as
"Colorless green ideas sleep furiously," Chomsky (1957a:15)
saw grammatical but nonsensical constructions which ques-
tioned the feasibility of a semantic foundation of grammar.
Jakobson (1959c:SW II 494f.) objected that, in contradistinction to totally agrammatical configurations such as
"Furiously sleep ideas green colorless," the above sentence,
like many figurative formulations of poetry, can still be
submitted to a truth test.

> The analysis of grammatical transformations and of their import
> should include the poetic function of language, because the core
> of this function is to push transformations into the foreground. It
> is the purposeful poetic use of lexical and grammatical tropes and
> figures that brings the creative power of language to its summit.
> (1972a:80)

Tropes and figures have an established, incontestable
place in poetics. In philosophy, on the other hand, they have
long been contested. Do different linguistic forms correspond
to different forms in reality? In settling this philosophical
dispute, Jakobson goes back to Franz Brentano and the
"Theory of Fictions" of the English thinker, Jeremy
Bentham (1748-1832). "To language, then—to language
alone—it is that fictitious entities owe their existence; their
impossible, yet indispensable existence" (Bentham, quoted
by Jakobson, 1961b:598). Moreover, with Bentham's thesis,
Jakobson disclaims the realistic conception of linguistic
figures as well as the philosophical decisionism which regards
these figures as arbitrary posits which can be entirely
transferred into formal, logical language. Figures are indispensable. In more recent publications, Jakobson has made
increasing reference to the acute distinction of the *modi
significandi* ("modes of signifying") made by medieval
scholasticism (1975b; see Pinborg, 1967). The expressions (1)
"The bird flies superbly" and (2) "The bird's flight is superb"
refer to the same fact, but make a distinction between (1) *per*

modum fluxus ("in the mode of an event") and (2) *per modum permanentis* ("in the mode of a state"). Sapir (quoted by Jakobson, 1961b:598) would translate the Latin as "modes of occurrence and existence."

While Jakobson, in the tradition of Brentano and Bentham, repudiates the reification of figures, he also unequivocally opposes the leveling of differences in meaning which arise from transformations. The active and passive formulation of an occurrence—(1) "The hunter killed the lion" and (2) "The lion was killed by the hunter"—are only similar but not the same in meaning. The passive transformation shifts the semantic perspective from the agent to the target of the action. The change is also revealed by the fact that in (1) the object ("the lion") and in (2) the agent ("by the hunter") may be omitted without rendering the sentence nonsensical (1959c:SW II 489; 1972a:78). Besides such contextual modifications of meaning, there are also stylistic modifications. The former deal with the cognitive content of the information, the latter with its emotive aspect. In Czech, use of the personal pronoun accompanying the verb (*já jedu* 'I drive') is a pleonasm and is felt to express a boastful style. In everyday speech, the verb with its ending, which indicates the person, suffices. It is just the opposite in Russian. The verb alone (*edu* instead of *ja edu*) does not necessarily reveal the person. Here it is the omission of the pronoun that makes a high-flown impression (1939d:SW II 217f.).

The disregard of such variations in meaning is one objection that Jakobson makes to Chomskian transformational grammar. Another is the hierarchy of syntactic structures; on the one hand, the status of deep structures, on the other, the ranking order of structures. In syntax as in phonology and morphonology, Jakobson does not recur to posited deep structures containing abstract elements, i.e., elements which occur in no surface structure or actualized utterance. The construction of abstract deep structures presents a phenomenologically unwarranted multiplication of entities. Jakobson adheres to the actual utterances of a language and seeks to define their interrelations. It is found that the hierarchy defined by the informational content of utterances displays an astonishing coincidence with the genetic hierarchy, the mastery of these utterances by the growing child. Jakobson has exposed the oppositional pair marked/unmarked, which we shall treat in more detail in section 2.5.3., as the most important ordering principle.

Such empirically demonstrable facts are often neglected by adherents of transformational grammar. Thus, they impute a deep structure, in which the adjective functions as predicate, to the attributive use of the adjective. The best-known example is the sentence *Dieu invisible a créé le monde visible* ("Invisible God created the visible world"), analyzed by the Port-Royal *Grammaire* and taken over by Chomsky (1966:33ff.) in illustration of his own conception. Chomsky, like the grammarians of the seventeenth century, derives the above sentence (3) from three simple sentences (1) *Dieu est invisible, Le monde est visible, Dieu a créé le monde* via an intermediate form (2) *Dieu QUI est invisible a créé le monde QUI est visible.* This does not, however, reflect the natural sequence of the syntactic use of the adjective. The simplest form is the attributive (3), followed by the plain predicative (1), and not until much later by the relative clause (2) (cf. Jakobson's analysis [1939d:SW II 216] of the Latin *Deus bonus – Deus bonus est,* "God is good"). Husserl's (1939:124ff.) investigations on transcendental logic, concerned with the genesis of logical evidences, confirm Jakobson's thesis. Attribution of properties or separation of accidents from a substance, called explication by Husserl, is a more original, more fundamental "logical" achievement than predication, which the Port-Royal grammarians and Chomsky (1966:33) consider "the principal form of thought." Another example is the derivation of the imperative ("Go!") from assertive and declarative sentences ("You will go," "I order you to go"). Together with the vocative, the imperative is the earliest form to appear in child language while pronouns such as *I* and *you,* auxiliary verbs such as *will* and performative verbs such as *order* are quite late acquisitions. That the earliest category of child language should be a complicated transformation of structures that make a much later appearance seems most unlikely from a psychological point of view (1972a:80). A possible metalingual explication is mistakenly equated with the code, the actual competence of the young speaker.

2.4.2.5. *Inventory of elements vs. system of rules.* Many critics see the exclusive achievement of taxonomic linguistics in the establishment of inventories of linguistic elements and their fixed patterns, while the primary aim should in fact be "the intricate system of rules by which these patterns are formed, modified, and elaborated" (Chomsky, 1972a:75). On the background of these systems of rules, the structural patterns appear as secondary, as a "kind of epiphenomenon."*

In this critique, Jakobson's phonological studies are ceded the merit of having demonstrated that all phonological systems build upon an astonishingly small number of universal features. The initiator of the critique, Chomsky, is more reserved and less absolutist in the confrontation with the phonology developed by Prague structuralism than many of those who come after him. Thus, he recognizes the organic, i.e., dynamic and creative, character of Trubetzkoy and Jakobson's phonological systems and their explanatory procedure (Chomsky, 1964:30; 1966:26). And indeed, Trubetzkoy and Jakobson's statements in this regard are perfectly unambiguous.† "A phonological system is not a

---

*The assignment of the term *taxonomy* to a scientific movement thought to be content with an inventorial accumulation is not very felicitous. The term is composed of the Greek words *táxis* 'arrangement' and *nómos* 'rule, law' and properly designates a theory aimed at the explanation of an order in terms of its laws. This original meaning of the word is one reason for our continued use of it to characterize Jakobson's linguistics, in spite of its currently misleading implications.

†In outspoken contrast to American culture and science, Russian culture and science are thoroughly antipositivistic.

The Russian milieu could well be called hostile to positivism. It suffices to state that the heyday of positivism in Russia was qualitatively rather mediocre, whereas contemporaneous oppositional lines of development, especially in the field of Russian philosophy, burst into magnificent bloom (Danilevskij, Dostoevskij, Fedorov, Leont'ev, Soloviev). The aversion to positivism characterizes all products of Russian thought—from Dostoevskij

mechanical sum of isolated phonemes, but an organic whole
of which the phonemes are members whose structure is
governed by laws" (Trubetzkoy, 1933:245).

In his major study on child language (1941), Jakobson
demonstrated that the patterning of the linguistic sound
system follows a strict order. The pattern, as has already been
stated, can be easily formalized: if *a* is given, then *b* is also
given; if *c* is not given, then *d* is not given either; and so on.
After outlining the stratification which is governed by these
laws of implication, the book details in the next chapter the
"Foundation [*Begründung* 'explanation'] of the Structural
Laws," opening with the following declaration: "The stratification of components in a phonemic system proves to be
strictly regular. These laws can be *explained,* however, only
by considering and demonstrating their inner necessity"
(1941:SW I 373).

The explanation of the laws is undertaken in "an
inherently linguistic and comprehensive procedure." It can be
shown that the sequence of stages of the phonemic system
obeys "the principle of maximal contrast and proceeds from
the simple and undifferentiated to the stratified and differentiated" (ibid., 374). The simple, unmarked terms of a
pair of phonemes develop more easily than the differentiated,
marked terms.

> The first stage of child language begins with a clear distinction
> and delimitation of consonant and vowel.... From the motor
> point of view, these two fundamental classes of speech sounds are
> contrasted with each other as closure and opening. The optimal

---

to Russian Marxism. (1929d:633)

Russian linguistics is no exception. In commemoration of his teacher Jan V.
Porzeziński, Jakobson (1929e) writes:

I shall never forget what Jan V. Porzeziński said to me when we parted in
Moscow in the year 1920. We spoke of the crisis in European linguistics.
"It is terrible," he said, "facts and more facts are being accumulated
without knowing what for—nor what to do with them!" Without the
theoretical conception which shapes the material and without the search
for laws, there was no science for the faithful disciple of Fortunatov and of
the Russian scientific tradition.

opening is achieved in the wide *a*-vowel, while among the stop consonants it is the labial sounds which obstruct the entire oral cavity. One might postulate that just this most simple and maximal contrast is qualified to inaugurate the distinction between the vocalic and consonantal systems at the threshold of child language, and in fact this hypothesis is confirmed by experience. (ibid., 375)

The most varied psychological explanations have been proffered for the child's familiar early linguistic formations *mama* and *papa*. Jakobson concurs to a certain extent with the derivation of *mama* from sucking activity and from the affective content of the prelinguistic nasal murmur. The /p/ in *papa* has a deictic, indicative function. It is significant that this sound, which signals the transition from the affective babbling stage to designative speech, appears in the term reserved for the male parent (1941:SW I 377f.; 1960d: 542f.). Beyond such psychological argumentation, Jakobson, for the first time, tenders a systematic, structural explanation of the infant's vocabulary in intrinsically linguistic terms.

A typology—*typology* is the current linguistic term corresponding to what in biology is called taxonomy—which is content with a mere listing of randomly amassed components and which does not take logical and economical criteria (problems of redundancy) into account inevitably leads to a distorted picture of language, devoid of all comparative usefulness. But such is not Jakobson's method. "Not Inventory but System Is Base of Typology" (Subtitle, 1958b:SW I 524); "The universal and near-universal laws of implication which underlie this taxonomy reveal a rigorous phonemic and grammatical stratification. . . ." (1962e:SW II 284).

2.4.2.6. *Observation and description vs. explanation.* Chomsky (1964:28ff.) reproves the behavioristically oriented, American brand of structuralism for not going beyond correct coverage and classification of observable linguistic data. Chomsky demands more from a linguistic theory than observational adequacy. It must also deliver a grammar which provides the system of rules upon which speaker and listener rely in making and understanding an utterance. Chomsky calls a grammar that satisfies this postulate descriptively adequate. This may be misleading because such a grammar is basically "an explanatory theory" (Chomsky, 1972a:27). However, Chomsky wishes to reserve the term *explanatory adequacy* for a linguistics that goes a step further and examines why the speaker and hearer of a language or the linguist who studies the language have chosen precisely this grammar and no other. The choice of grammar should be founded on the structure of the human mind. With this approach, linguistics according to Chomsky, becomes a "subfield of psychology," while structural linguistics is accused of a "militant anti-psychologism" (ibid., 28, 65).

Chomsky's outline is of only limited usefulness in the presentation of the problematic of explanation vs. description as posed and solved by Prague structuralism. Prague structuralism evolved out of a deliberate renunciation of a particular brand of explanatory linguistics, that of the neogrammarians. Neogrammarian explanations are characterized by two properties. They are causal-genetic and heterogeneous in nature. In explaining linguistic events, the neogrammarians recurred to antecedent, nonlinguistic events, interpreted as causing the former. Well into the twentieth century, headway in research was shackled by the fixation on outgrowths of late scholastic philosophy. With the repudiation of this philosophy, the mechanistic sciences of modern times launched their march to triumph. They continued to suspect that *idem-per-idem* explanations, similar to the *vis-dormitiva* tautology of the late Middle Ages which explained the soporific effect of poppy by its soporific force, lurked behind pure description. The Prague linguists responded to the epistemological restriction (only genetic explanations) and confusion (eclectic, heterogeneous explanations) of the neogrammarians with a multilevel and balanced concept. In addition to the genetic "why?", they raised both the descriptive question "how?" and the functional question "what for?".

The descriptive, properly structural portion of Prague

linguistics is characterized by (1) emphasis on the autonomy of linguistics and (2)—what at first sight may seem paradoxical—the explanatory role ascribed to just these structural linguistics.

The emphasis on the autonomy of linguistics and the rejection of precocious psychological explanations have earned Prague structuralism the censure of antipsychologism (cf. the shift of accent in the use of this catchword, antipsychologism, in Jakobson, 1939b:SW I 315; 1974e:16). It is easy to overlook that demonstration of the autonomy of linguistic laws by no means eliminates the psychological question. On the contrary, not until the nature of the system of language has been given due consideration can the psychological question be properly raised. And it no longer reads: how can individual, atomistic, linguistic phenomena be explained psychologically, but rather, what must the human mind be like to be capable of producing and receiving a system that is constituted upon specific, intrinsic laws?

Prague structuralism, in a remarkable historical duplication, shares with Husserl's phenomenology both the reproach of antipsychologism and the perspective from which the question of a psychological foundation is approached. The problematic merely shifts from the level of logic to that of linguistics. After Husserl, in the first volume of his *Logical Investigations*, had demonstrated that logical laws cannot be deduced from the factual nature of the human conscious, but are rather founded in the meaning of the fundamental logical concepts, he then formulated, at the beginning of the second volume (1913:254), the enduring psychological questions in the only acceptable form, namely:

How are we to understand the fact that the intrinsic being of objectivity becomes "presented," "apprehended" in knowledge, and so ends up by becoming subjective? What does it mean to say that the object has "intrinsic being" and is "given" in knowledge? How can the ideality of the universal *qua* concept or law enter the flux of real mental states and become an epistemic possession of the thinking person?

The question as to the "innateness" of linguistic laws remains largely speculative. The real problem lies in the elucidation of "the internal logic of linguistic structures" (Jakobson, 1974e:48). What is founded in the logic of a phenomenon itself presupposes no special "genetic instructions" (a phenomenological example: the embeddedness of a present perception in a past and future horizon; a linguistic example: the priority of the attributive over the predicative assignment of the adjective to the noun). Characteristic of "a priori" linguistic laws is the individual speaker's possibility of ignoring them in verbal plays and novel turns of phrase (as in "forbidden" formulations such as "John does not play golf; golf plays John" (Jakobson, 1959c:SW II 495; cf. Chomsky, 1957a:42).

Structural description is in Prague linguistics no end in itself—even as it is not in biological taxonomy. The neglect of this fact is one of the most unforgivable failings of the fashionable taxonomy criticism. The proper goal of taxonomic classification is pithily summed up in a statement of the biologist G. G. Simpson (1964:11): "Classificatory language is to have primarily evolutionary significance."

In the biological theory of evolution, the taxonomic base was long concealed through the repression of classical morphological terminology by a genealogical vocabulary. Instead of systematics one spoke of phylogenetics; instead of form affinity, of blood affinity; instead of systematic series of stages, of series of ancestors; instead of type, of the form of genealogical trees (*Stammform*); instead of typical states, of original ones; instead of atypical states, of modified ones; instead of lower animals, of primitive ones; instead of derivation, of descent; and so on (Naef, 1919:35f.). Contemporary biological taxonomy has once again awakened to the fact that only a minute portion of evolution is directly observable; for the vast remainder recourse is taken to typological criteria. Phylogenetic classification rests on a phenomenological classification (Sokal and Sneath, 1963).

In a lecture significantly entitled "Typological Studies and their Contribution to Historical Comparative Linguistics"

(1958b:SW I 523ff.), Jakobson summed up the analogous import of taxonomic classification for linguistics. Typology, alias taxonomy, supplies the criteria for the reconstruction of linguistic stages of the past. Certain stages of development are quite likely, others less so, and still others virtually impossible. Furthermore, in addition to its heuristic value, linguistic taxonomy also has an explanatory value. This discovery induced the young Jakobson, in 1926, to send off an "excited" letter to Trubetzkoy, "raising the question whether it might not be conceivable to bridge the unnatural chasm between synchronic analysis of the phonological system, on the one hand, and 'historical phonetics', on the other, by examining each sound change as a purposive phenomenon from the point of view of the total system" (1939c:SW II 512f.). It was this insight that first motivated the language historian Trubetzkoy to direct his attention toward systematic phonology.

Along with the idea of system, the Prague linguists introduced a functional perspective into linguistics. The functional, teleological, or, still better, teleonomical explanation is the mode of explanation and the criterion for evaluation which predominates in Prague structuralism. Linguistics demands this kind of explanatory adequacy. This can be illustrated by the concept of the phoneme, the binarism of the distinctive features, and sound change. The most worthwhile sound analysis is the one that does greatest justice to the function of linguistic sounds, which lies in differentiating meaning. It is primarily function that illuminates the system of rules according to which linguistic patterns are shaped and reshaped and that endows the system with an inner necessity.

The regard for the various "functional dialects", or, in other words, the different styles of language radically altered the view of linguistic change. The two stages of a change in progress were reinterpreted as two simultaneous styles of language; the change was conceived as a fact of linguistic synchrony, and as any fact of synchrony it demanded a means-ends test with respect to the whole system of language. Thus historical linguistics experienced a complete metamorphosis. If in the previous stage of Indo-European studies, as Benveniste stated in 1935, "l'effort, considérable et méritoire, qui a été employé à la description des formes n'a été suivi d'aucune tentative sérieuse pour les interpréter", henceforth, he pointed out, it would be necessary ... to envisage the functions of the elements involved. (1963b:SW II 525)*

2.4.3. *Teleonomy.* The Moscow and Prague linguists championed the right and necessity of the teleological explanation long before it was rehabilitated by cybernetics and by its application especially in biology. Teleological thinking is deeply rooted in Russian ideology.

The imbalance toward the "what for" as against the "why" is typical of Russian thought. Vinogradov is right in emphasizing the teleological bias of Russian thought in the persons of its greatest representatives. An anti-Darwinist tendency runs through the Russian philosophy of nature like a leitmotif. Apart from the German Baer, who is inseparably linked with Russian science, it suffices to mention the argumentations of Danilevskij, Strachov, Vavilov, and Berg, which have today crystallized into the harmonious doctrine of nomogenesis permeated by the idea of goal-directedness. The category of mechanistic causality is foreign to Russian thinking. (1929d:633)

For a logical conception of teleology going beyond the old philosophy of nature, Jakobson (1933:SW II 544) was able, to a certain degree, to profit from his colleague in Brno, economist Karel Engliš. After the Second World War, Jakobson recurred to the successful cybernetic approach of biology (1974e:55ff.; 1974b). To avoid stubborn misunderstandings, he acclaimed biologist C. S. Pittendrigh's suggestion that the new conception of finality be distinguished from the old, metaphysical idea of a final cause through the neologism teleonomy, just as the distinction is made between scientific astronomy and speculative astrology.

*Cf. Jakobson's reference to parallel functional explanations in biological taxonomy and evolutionary theory (1929a:SW I 107; 1974e:46).

Although Engliš (1930) still maintained that purpose refers back to a subject, he achieved an admirable formalization of teleology. According to him, teleology is not a psychological fact, but a logical form of explanation. It is a form of intuition by means of which experience is perceived and apprehended, comparable to the Kantian spatial form of intuition, which also delivers forms with which the real world can be grasped. The causal form of thought, as it burst forth in classical physics, arranges events in terms of cause and effect; the teleological form of thought, in terms of means and ends. The base idea in the first case is force; in the second, utility or function.

Recent discussion makes a fundamental distinction between goal-intended and goal-directed behavior. Goal-intended behavior is based on conscious ideas, convictions, wishes, and intentions. These act as the cause of a particular behavior. With regard to this behavior, it is not so much the type of causal nexus as the ontological status of ideas and wishes which is considered problematic by philosophers who accept only the externally observable. Should the existence of ideas and wishes be accepted, then the teleological explanation easily allows reduction to a special, psychical form of causality; in this case, the behavior is not explained by something in the future, but rather by something in the present, by current ideas and intentions. A process is designated as goal-directed when it evokes the appearance of goal-intended behavior but no consciously acting subject is discernable. Since many functions of language are unconscious, they cannot simply be thrown in with the less problematic goal-intended processes, but must be explained as goal-directed processes.

The criterion for teleonomic processes was originally thought to have been found in "behavioral plasticity," through which a certain state is achieved in the course of changing circumstances. However, although a river flows into the sea with almost proverbial adaptation to circumstance and resistance, talk of a goal-directed course hardly seems justified. The criterion of "directive correlation" proves to be more valid. A process is regarded as teleonomic when it is bound to another process in such a way that it not only causes it, but is in turn steered in its own course by the other process. Such a directive correlation must be assumed when the result of a process represents a system characterized by certain formal properties (gestalt qualities) such as simplicity, balance, and symmetrical and hierarchical arrangement, or when the process reveals itself to be a condition for the normal course of a more comprehensive process of which it is an integrated part. Well-known biological illustrations are, in the first case, the development of symmetrical forms (e.g., the shape of leaves) and, in the second case, heart action in vertebrates. In language, the restitution of a sound system that has become imbalanced and the emergence of phonological, distinctive features without meaning in themselves but constituting meaningful units, morphemes and words, can be cited as examples of this phenomenon.

The characteristic formal criterion of a goal-directed process lies in the fact that a holistic system can be discovered as a determining or explanatory factor of its parts. A variable event E_1 is not only dependent, i.e., a function in the mathematical sense of the word, upon other variable events E_2, E_3, ..., E_n, but also and primarily upon a system S. The single event cannot be understood unless the system has been extricated: $E_1 = f(S; E_2, E_3, ..., E_n)$. In this sense, the structural and functional methods are not two heterogeneous procedures, which simply happened to collide externally and historically in the *Cercle linguistique de Prague* due to the simultaneous influence of Saussure and Baudouin de Courtenay. Both methods classify the elements of a set as parts of a whole.

The Prague linguists characteristically defend the basically functional character of language and also stress the diversity of linguistic functions (CLP, 1929:7, 14f.; Jakobson, 1963b:SW II 522ff.). A structural conception, in the narrow sense of the word, has been championed by representatives of American structuralism under the heading of distributionalism, according to which the arrangement of elements in language is defined exclusively by context. In contradistinction, Jakobson defends language as a means of designation. "The primary function of the sign is to signify and not to figure in certain given constellations" (1949c:38). The mathematical concept of function, which expresses a purely formal relation of dependence, must not be allowed to suppress the sociological concept of function in linguistics—function interpreted as purpose and role (ibid.).

The pragmatic tendency is to concentrate too exclusively on everyday speech in which the use of language as a means of communication dominates, while the Prague linguists bring the diversity of linguistic functions into play. Their alert responsiveness to this diversity is due chiefly to their familiarity with literature and poetry, where it is the aesthetic orientation towards the *signans* that dominates and not the communicative orientation towards the *signatum*. The system of linguistic functions will be outlined in 3.2.

2.5. *Opposition*

Structure is a widely used and, according to some, threadbare term that is no longer of much value in distinguishing one scientific trend from other, competing ones. Roland Barthes (1963:213) therefore suggests resorting to "pairings like those of *signifier/signified* and *synchronic/diachronic* in order to approach what distinguishes structuralism from other modes of thought: the first because it refers to the linguistic model as originated by Saussure . . . ; the second . . . because it seems to imply a certain revision of the notion of history. . . ." Jakobson seems to prefer a more fundamental criterion even if, as a result, the majority of current scientific trends falls under the heading of structuralism. The discovery of just such common ground surprised the Prague linguists. In their search for procedural modes which do justice to the specific laws of language, they came upon methods that they found were being simultaneously developed by the avant-garde of the most varied scientific disciplines. What united them all was repudiation of the mechanistic atomization of facts by disclosing the interdependence among the components of a whole and between the whole and its components.

The main feature of structuralism, according to Jakobson, is the cardinal role assigned to the most important relation that has been extracted by structural linguistics, that of opposition, understood as the reciprocal implication of two contrary or contradictory terms.

> The former arguments for a mechanical and impervious compartmentalization of linguistics and the dogma of irremovable antinomies gradually yield to a comprehensive inquiry into the vital unity of opposites, such as autonomy and integration, statics and dynamics, concurrence and sequence, code and message, contiguity and similarity, token and value, form and substance, grammar and semantics, meaning and reference, object- and meta-language, inter- and intra-communication, invariance and variation, creation and diffusion, particularism and conformism, etc. (1975c)

We have already discussed some of these oppositions. We shall now treat the structure of opposition as such and one of its most remarkable modes, the opposition marked/unmarked.

2.5.1. *The phenomenological definition of opposition.* The core of Saussure's *Cours de linguistique générale* is often seen in the doctrine of value (1916:111ff.). Linguistic signs do not owe their value to a positive, absolute character, but to their relative position within a system. The definition of the phoneme in the *Cours* (119) is familiar: "Phonemes are above all else oppositive, relative, and negative entities." In spite of the fundamental role of the terms *difference* and *opposition*, Saussure does not define their relation consistently and unambiguously. Following the Dutch phenomenologist Hendrik Pos, Jakobson set about to elucidate them and has introduced a precise definition of opposition.

Opposition is a binary relation in which one term "univocally, reversibly, and necessarily" calls for another (1949a:SW I 421). *Light* evokes another specific term, *dark*.

The evocation is reversible. *Dark* calls for *light* as well. The evocation is indispensable. *Light* cannot be thought without *dark*. This condition is fulfilled by two kinds of difference: contradictory and contrary (1939e:SW I 273). A contradictory difference exists between the presence and absence of an element or a feature (the relation vocalic/nonvocalic). A contrary difference is given in the relation between two elements which belong to the same genus and are maximally distinct from one another within this genus (the extreme elements in the periodic system of chemistry) or which are realized in the maximum or minimum of a feature which displays a graduated scale. Contrary opposition is also called polar opposition (black/white).

These two kinds of difference, the only ones which Jakobson designates as opposition, are not to be confounded with simple or "contingent" differences in which the givenness of a term allows no prediction about the nature of its partner. If someone says "I see a meadow," then we do not know from what he distinguishes it—from a forest, a lake, a cliff, or whatever. Unlike *light, meadow* has no definite opposing partner.

Almost simultaneously with Saussure, gestalt psychology proposed a duality as the fundamental notion of perception: the relation of figure and background. To perceive a figure, a contingent difference from the background suffices. We can perceive a city on the background of the countryside just as well as on the background of a lake. Gestalt psychology made little effort to further illuminate the concept of difference, with one exception. In the case of sensory qualities, gestalt psychology had already determined that the quality of the background affects the quality of the figure in a very specific direction. Colors illustrate this most clearly. The color of the background brings about a change in the direction of the complementary color of its figure. A grey body appears greenish on a red background and yellowish on a blue one. The color of a figure is more intense the more it stands in contrast to the color of its background. The effect of red is most intense against green, its complementary color.

The effect consists of an enlargement or optimalization of the difference in the direction of the contrary opposition.

Gestalt psychology was primarily concerned with natural systems of perception. The phonological system of linguistics, on the other hand, is an artifact. In its build-up, the tendency of natural systems of perception to form optimal oppositions is fully exploited. The exploitation of this tendency is functionally motivated. The function of phonemes consists in the differentiation of meanings. They best fulfill this end when they are themselves optimally distinguished from each other, i.e., through the contrary or contradictory opposition of their distinctive features. Opposition is an excellent model for confronting a purely logical description of structure with a phenomenological one. In treatises on logic, opposition is consistently defined as formal exclusion. The proponents of a positivistic logicism in linguistics assume this definition: "For monemes, as well as for phonemes, membership in one and the same system implies opposition, i.e., *exclusive choice*" (Martinet, 1960:4.8.).

A phenomenological analysis differs from a purely logical one by not only examining each datum as it is "in itself," but also as it is given in the conscious, "for us." From this phenomenological point of view, opposition appears as both an exclusion and an inclusion. In the conscious as well, oppositions such as light and dark exclude each other, but the excluded term of the opposition is necessarily co-given in the conscious.

> Opposition . . . always unites two things which are distinct but, at the same time, connected in such a way that thought cannot posit the one without the other. The unity of opposites is always formed by a concept which implicitly contains them in itself and becomes divided into an explicit opposition when it is applied to concrete reality. . . . Opposition in linguistic facts is not a scheme which science has introduced to master the facts and which remains external to them. Its import surpasses the epistemological sphere: when linguistic thought orders the facts according to

principles of opposition and system, it encounters a thinking which itself creates these facts. (Pos, 1938:246; Jakobson, 1949a: SW I 423)

Opposition ... is not a relation that is observed but one that thinks itself. ... From the point of view of content, nothing could be more distinct: white differs more from black than yellow does. But from the point of view of thought, nothing could be more connected, more inseparable: the one implies the other. ... (Pos, 1939a:75f.; see Jakobson, 1939a:SW I 301)

The psychological reality of opposition, its immanence in the human mind, is further demonstrated by the fact that the formation of oppositional pairs precedes the constitution of isolated objects and appears as the first logical operation of the child (Wallon, 1945; Jakobson, 1962a:SW I 649). With his revised version of the notion of opposition, Jakobson (1939a:SW I 294f., 301ff.) subjects Saussure's oppositive definition of linguistic signs to a two-fold critique. First, he objects to its mechanistic transference from phonology to other linguistic levels. True, a phoneme has no other sign value than that of indicating otherness. In the words *talk* and *walk,* the phonemes /t/ and /w/ signalize the presence of two distinct words with different meanings. All the remaining linguistic signs, on the other hand, signalize more than mere otherness. They have a positive value. The morpheme *s* in *days* and *nights* indicates plurality in both cases. Saussure's assertion (1916:122) that "when isolated, neither 'night' nor 'nights' is anything: thus everything is opposition" is not tenable. The prerequisite of the designative faculty of the sign, its systematic difference from other signs, must not be confused with the designation itself. The existence of the plural presupposes that of the singular. But the decisive factor for the plural morpheme, the justification for its existence, is its own positive value, the designation of plurality.

Second, a revision is necessary within phonology itself. This revision does not, as in the first point of the criticism, concern the *differentiating* function of signs, but their *differing* structure. An oppositional relation in the proper, strict sense of the word, does not stand between phonemes, but only between the distinctive features of phonemes.

> Let us, for instance, examine the relation between two vowel phonemes /u/ and /a/. The one can doubtless be thought without calling for the appearance of the other. The manifold oppositional terms are the same in *one* respect: the terms, mother and father, day and night, expensive and cheap, big and small, presuppose each other. This is not the case with the phonemes /u/ and /a/. . . .
>   . . . The oppositions of distinctive features are real, logical, binary oppositions, and each term of these oppositions necessarily includes its opposing partner. Wideness cannot be thought without narrowness, back formation without front formation, rounded without unrounded, etc. (1939a:SW I 301, 303)

Later, Jakobson (1962a:SW I 637) was to point out that his criticism applies not to Saussure himself but only to the editors of the *Cours,* who deviated here as elsewhere from his actual teachings. In the original records of Saussure's lectures (1967ff.:268), not "phonemes" but "elements" are assigned a purely oppositive, relative, and negative value.

2.5.2. *The confirmation of binarism by the theory of information.* Jakobson's focus on opposition as the fundamental structure of the phonological level and, to a certain extent, of the other linguistic levels as well has repeatedly met with fierce condemnation. Jakobson and his students have been accused of violating linguistic reality as a consequence of their subjective, arbitrary research, on the one extreme, or rigid adherence to system, on the other. One critic (Joos, 1957:415) views Jakobson's binary structuration of language as a "polar metaphor," which as such is "a literary performance of high merit," but has at most a certain heuristic usefulness for science.

Yet Jakobson, for his phonemic analysis, draws on a science to which one would hardly ascribe literary ambitions. The mathematical theory of communication has with striking success demonstrated that any set of data can not only in principle be analyzed through binary decisions, but further that this mode of analysis exhibits the greatest efficiency. Phonology and the theory of communication have independently arrived at similar, mutually complementary conclusions, leading to a fruitful cooperation between the two (1956a:SW I 497; 1961a:SW II 570ff.).

Thus Jakobson, together with his student Morris Halle and the London communications theorist E. Colin Cherry, undertook an exemplary logical description of the phonological side of language, based on the phonological system in Russian (1953c:SW I 449ff.). For the most economical identification of the object H from among a set of eight abstract objects A, B, . . . , H (see Fig. 6), the whole group is split into two equal halves. One can then pose the question: does H belong to the right side or not? The side to which H belongs is split again and the question repeated on the new level until the object has been identified. Instead of having to put a maximum of eight questions (Is it A? Is it B?, etc.), only three questions answered by "yes" (+) or "no" (-) suffice in this example. The answers for H yield a chain (+++). The number of "yes"-"no" answers for N objects is equivalent to $\log_2 N$.

A	B	C	D	E	F	G	H
−	−	−	−	+	+	+	+
−	−	+	+	−	−	+	+
−	+	−	+	−	+	−	+

(1953c: SW I 453)

Figure 6

Phonology deals not with abstract objects but with concrete elements, whose structure is determined by the mode of production and reception by speaker and listener. Consequently, identification no longer follows from abstract questions (right or left?), but rather from questions as to the phonic character of the elements (vocalic or not? compact or diffuse? etc.). Thereby, even in the first question, most systems do not split into two equal groups. The forty-two phonemes in Russian, for instance, yield twelve pluses and thirty minuses. Nor can all questions apply to all phonemes, be it that the identification is already complete without them, or that they would imply an impossible articulation. The answer in these cases is indefinite (o). Thus, a three-valued logic is required for the identification of phonemes. As a result, a phoneme in Russian cannot be identified by the ideal logical average of 5.38 questions, but necessitates up to 11 questions. For the so-called consonants in English, this procedure yields plus, minus, and zero answers as in Figure 7.

	p	t	č	k	b	d	ǰ	g	f	s	θ	š	v	z	đ	ž	m	n	ŋ
consonantal/noncons.	+	+	+	+	+	+	+	+	+	+	+	+	+	+	+	+	+	+	+
vocalic/nonvocalic	-	-	-	-	-	-	-	-	-	-	-	-	-	-	-	-	-	-	-
nasal/nonnasal	-	-	-	-	-	-	-	-	-	-	-	-	-	-	-	-	+	+	+
compact/diffuse	-	-	+	+	-	-	+	+	-	-	-	+	-	-	-	+	-	-	+
grave/acute	+	-			+	-			+	-	-		+	-	-		+	-	
continuant/abrupt	-	-	-	-	-	-	-	-	+	+	+	+	+	+	+	+			
tense/lax	+	+	+	+	-	-	-	-	+	+	+	+	-	-	-	-			
strident/mellow			+	-			+	-		+	-			+	-				

Figure 7*

The process of identification can be abridged if the questions that remain open for each phoneme are transferred to the bottom of the list, so that they can be eliminated as

---

*Linda R. Waugh kindly set up the table of English consonants for this study. Zero answers are indicated by blank spaces.
č as in "*ch*ur*ch*" (may also be written as c)
ǰ as in "*j*u*dg*e" (may also be written as j)
š as in "*sh*ine" (may also be written as ʃ)
ž as in "rou*g*e" (may also be written as ʒ)
θ as in "*th*in"
đ as in "*th*en" (may also be written as δ)
ŋ as in "si*ng*

soon as the phoneme has been sufficiently identified. To this end, the order of the questions in the course of the identification process must be modified. The change is not arbitrary, but dependent upon the answers to the preceding questions. Thus, in Russian, if the reply to the first two questions (vocalic? consonantal?) is positive, one can immediately proceed to the ninth question (strident?) and then back to the seventh (continuant?) in order to identify the phonemes /r/ — /r,/ — /l/ — /l,/. Since the response to the first two questions is positive, only these four phonemes are possible. With this procedure, the number of questions in Russian no longer amounts to 11, but to an average of 6.5, which comes very close to the logical ideal value of 5.38. The number can be still further reduced by taking into account the dependence of the phonemes on their context, i.e., the preceding phonemes and groups of phonemes as well as the grammatical categories in which they are embedded.

2.5.3. *The opposition marked/unmarked.* A special form of opposition is the relation marked/unmarked, one of the most striking phenomena in the construction of language. Trubetzkoy and Jakobson have written on it since the early thirties (a first discovery of this relation can be found in Jakobson, 1921a:132 [n. 16]). For some time now, modern linguistics (Greenberg, 1966; Chomsky and Halle, 1968:402ff.) and psycholinguistics (Clark, 1970; 1973) have also applied themselves to this phenomenon. In Jakobson's linguistics, the dyad marked/unmarked together with the dyad variation/invariance play a role comparable to the principles of arbitrariness and linearity in Saussure's system (1916:67ff.).

> Whatever level of language we deal with, two integral properties of linguistic structure force us to use strictly relational, topological definitions. First, every single constituent of any linguistic system is built on an opposition of two logical contradictories: the presence of an attribute ("markedness") in contraposition to its absence ("unmarkedness"). The entire network of language displays a hierarchical arrangement that within each level of the system follows the same dichotomous principle of marked terms

superposed on the corresponding unmarked terms. And second, the continual, all-embracing, purposeful interplay of invariants and variations proves to be an essential, innermost property of language at each of its levels. (1972a:76)

The paired terms marked/unmarked were introduced by Trubetzkoy (1931:97):

The two terms of a correlative opposition (e.g., voiced/unvoiced) are not equivalent; the one term possesses the mark in question (or possesses it in its positive form), the other does not possess it (or possesses it in its negative form). We designate the first as marked, the second as unmarked.

Of importance here is Trubetzkoy's supplementary explication. The separation of an oppositive pair into a marked and an unmarked term does not rest on an "arbitrary, subjective estimation"; it is an "objective fact" expressed by specific properties.

Jakobson (1932b:SW II 3ff.; 1936b:SW II 29ff.; 1939d:SW II 211ff.; etc.; see also 1974d) took the marked/unmarked pair from phonology and applied it to morphology and syntax, whereby he elaborated Trubetzkoy's definition more precisely. In Trubetzkoy, the relation marked/unmarked is reduced to a "privative opposition," the presence vs. the absence of a mark (Trubetzkoy, 1939:67). The Geneva school, under the heading *signe zéro* "zero sign", also restricted its treatment of these phenomena to a privative relation. According to Saussure (1916:86), language can operate with the opposition between something and nothing. Thus, many languages distinguish the nominative not by a special, additional morpheme, but by the absence of one, while the other cases are marked by a special ending added on to the stem.

The complex structure of unmarked terms, which is inconspicuously expressed by the phenomenon of neutralization on the phonological level, makes an explicit appearance in morphology and syntax. The unmarked sign can have two distinct meanings—a general meaning and a restricted, "specific" one. The general meaning of the unmarked sign reveals nothing about the presence or absence of a—positive or negative!—property *P*. In its specific meaning, on the other hand, it signals the absence of a property, while the marked sign signals its presence (1932b:SW II 15; 1957:SW II 136).

marked term: statement of *P*

unmarked term: (1) general meaning: nonstatement of *P*
                               (2) specific meaning: statement of non-*P*

> The Russian word *oslíca* 'female donkey' signals that the animal is female, whereas the general meaning of the word *osël* 'donkey' contains no signalization of the sex of the intended animal. When I say *osël*, I do not specify whether I am talking about a male or a female, but if someone asks me, *eto oslíca*? 'Is it a female donkey?' and I reply, *nét, osël* 'No, a donkey', then the male sex has been signaled—the word is used in a narrowed sense. (1932b:SW II 4)

In comparison to the unmarked term, the marked term provides more information. This is best illustrated by the example of polar adjectives and nouns. The statement "Peter is as young as Paul" is more informative than the statement "Peter is as old as Paul." Someone unfamiliar with Paul's age knows, after the first statement, that he is relatively young while the second statement reveals nothing about his age. *Young* is the marked term, *old* the unmarked term. Two oppositions overlap in the relation marked/unmarked—the opposition between a positive and a negative term and between an indefinite and a definite one.

The phenomenon of neutralization is characteristic of the relation marked/unmarked on the level of meaning as well. If a language loses a term, then it is the marked one. In German, the future form of the verb is in the process of disappearing. The use of *Morgen fahre ich weg* ("Tomorrow I leave") is replacing *Morgen werde ich wegfahren* ("Tomorrow I will leave"). The future and past forms of the verb signal something, a definite time (or modality) not stated by the present form. They are more informative than the present, i.e., marked. Comparable to neutralization is the phenomenon of an optional use of the marked term in many contexts. The use of the unmarked term to signal its specific meaning is compulsory. For an event that is taking place now only the present tense may be used: "I understand." However, when reporting a historical event, we are not required to use the past tense. We can employ the historic present: "De Gaulle dies 1970." There are exceptions in which the marked term is used for the specific meaning of the unmarked term. The best-known example is the plural in formal address as in the German *Wie geht es Ihnen, Herr Adam*? ("How are you [pl.], Mr. Adam?"). This illustration displays an extended, metaphorical, one could also say marked, use of the marked term (1932b:SW II 4; 1972a: 80). On the other hand, the general meaning of the unmarked term cannot be considered an extended form of application. In the use of *goose* as a generic name for the female and male animal, there is no feeling of a figurative meaning as in the formal plural. For this reason the general meaning of the unmarked term is not defined as an extended form; rather, its specific meaning is defined as a restricted form.

Reduction to the unmarked term and optional use of the marked term are only two special cases of the general law, which asserts the priority of the unmarked sign in the build-up of language and the reverse priority of the marked sign in its aphasic break-down. This law applies on the ontogenetic and phylogenetic levels. The plural is marked in contrast to the singular. Within plural forms, the dual as the statement of a definite plurality is marked in contrast to the general, undefined plural. Hence, every child learns the singular first and then the plural. There is no language which manifests the dual without the plural. On the other hand, the aphasic first loses the plural and then the singular, and in languages with the dual, the dual disintegrates first as the more marked statement of number. If a language possesses only one of two oppositional terms, then it is the unmarked one. French disposes of two polar adjectives for spatial extension, *long* 'long' — *court* 'short', but possesses only the nominalization of the unmarked term: *longeur.* A marked oppositive term (as in English *shortness*) is lacking.

Another characteristic is that the unmarked term usually shows a simpler form on the side of the *signans* and a more complex form on the side of the *signatum.* In many languages, the plural is distinguished from the singular by an additional morpheme, while there seems to be no language in which this relation is reversed (1965b:SW II 352). On the phonological level, too, the marked term frequently exhibits the more complex form. German applies the umlaut, a marked phonological form, for the marked category of the plural in nouns (*Nacht—Nächte*) and for the marked comparative and superlative degrees in adjectives (*hoch— höher—am höchsten*). However, this characteristic is not universal. The relation can also be chiasmic (1939d:SW II 215). On the side of the *signatum,* the unmarked term of an opposition is often conspicuous through a greater differentiation. Frequently, pronouns, in English for example, are divided according to gender only in the unmarked third person singular, but not in the first and second persons singular or third person plural.

Besides these qualitative properties of the contrast marked/unmarked, quantitative properties can also be discerned. Statistical investigations have shown that the unmarked term is generally more frequent. Greenberg (1966:64ff.) would like to establish frequency as the chief criterion of markedness, not simply on methodological grounds because it is prevalent and can be grasped by mathematics and measured, but also because, in his opinion, frequency in the grammatical and semantic sphere is determined by the frequency of objects and situations sighted in the real world. In illustration of this, he states that *author* can mean a writer of both sexes, but *par excellence* a male writer, because in fact most authors are male. According to Jakobson, frequency is first and foremost a consequence of the fundamental law of the priority of the unmarked term in the development of language and the priority of the marked term in all the manifestations of its disintegration.

Neither does Jakobson stop at a mere description of the use of marked and unmarked terms. A linguistics whose ideal lies in explanatory adequacy must find out why the unmarked term is generally more frequently used, appears earlier in the build-up of language, is more resistant in its break-down, and is usually simpler as regards its outer form and more complex as regards its inner form. A mere description of the laws of use does not explain why the same entity displays unmarked behavior in some cases and marked behavior in others. A qualitative analysis of the *signans* or *signatum* is a prerequisite for explaining the use of marked and unmarked forms.

Only an analysis of the inner, "material," or qualitative structure can explain why the compactness of vowels is unmarked and their diffuseness marked, while the contrary holds for consonants. The nature of vowels is predominantly compact, that of consonants diffuse. Vocality and compactness are related features which mutually imply and reinforce each other. Vocalic and diffuse features, on the other hand, clash. Diffuseness encroaches upon vocality. The vowel /u/, which is diffuse in comparison with the optimal vowel /a/ (optimal in both the realization of vocality and in compactness), appears as a nonconforming, exceptional, and differentiated representative of its class, which explains the child's late acquisition of it and the aphasic's early loss (1960c:SW II 186; 1963a:SW II 582).

A qualitatively oriented explanation proves its fruitfulness in semantics as well. The potential two-fold employ of the unmarked term to designate the spatial dimension as such and to designate by contrast the extent of the dimension allows such sentences as "The short stick is four inches long," but not "The short stick is long." The concordance of the expression for the dimension of extension as such (*length*) with that which indicates "much" extension (*long*) and not with that which states "little" extension (*short*) is qualitatively motivated. The best way to make someone understand the dimension of length is by showing him a very long object.

This best separates length from other dimensions (width, height, etc.) (Clark, 1970:272ff.).

The reversibility of markedness can also be demonstrated in the sphere of semantics and "materially"-qualitatively explained. To this end, we compare the following sentences:

(1a) The north station is just as far from the center as the south station.

(1b) The north station is just as close to the center as the south station.

(2a) John is as closely associated with Mary as with Ann.

(2b) John is as loosely associated with Mary as with Ann.

(3a) John is as close (emotionally) to Mary as to Ann.

(3b) John is as far (emotionally) from Mary as from Ann.

(1a) gives us no information about the distance of the two stations from the center of the city; (1b) does. Similarly, (2a) and (3a) tell us nothing about the actual degree of John's relationship with the two girls, while (2b) and (3b) reveal that it cannot be very intimate.

What is striking here is that in (1b) and (3b) *close* and *far* are marked, i.e., more informative than their opposing terms, while in (1a), (2a), and (3a) they are unmarked, i.e., less informative. This inversion can be explained by examining the content of the words. In the first pair of sentences, the adjectives specify a spatial *extension*. The adjective which conforms more with that generic term, i.e., which indicates more extension than its polar, opposing partner, appears as unmarked. In the other two pairs of sentences, the genus specified is no longer an external distance, but an internal relationship, more precisely a *connection*. The maximal form of connection is unity. Hence, the expression that most nearly approaches it appears as unmarked. A restriction or negation of connectedness, on the other hand, results in markedness.

A semantics limited to the use of linguistic entities

proves inadequate. Similarly, a structuralism with a one-sided concentration on form and a disregard of "matter" as *quantité négligeable* does not satisfy. A linguistic structure as fundamental as the opposition marked/unmarked cannot be satisfactorily elucidated without recourse to the "material" or qualitative nature of phenomena.

3.
Perspectives of a Comprehensive Theory of Language

After presenting the philosophical principles which have—explicitly or implicitly—guided Jakobson's conception of structuralism, we now turn to the theory of language, whose building blocks have accumulated in Jakobson's hundreds of publications.* Its main characteristic is its comprehensiveness. Each linguistic aspect is assigned to its appropriate place in a hierarchically structured whole. Five perspectives in particular through which Jakobson describes and explains the data of language can be discerned. They are the axes, functions, and units of language, the phases of the speech act, and the interdisciplinary relations of linguistics.

---

*Certain repetitions and cross-references are unavoidable in this method-ological and thematically ordered interpretation of Jakobson's work. The original instigation for a separate and privileged treatment of the philosophically relevant methodological principles came from the request for an interpretation of Jakobson's work to appear not in a linguistic but in a philosophical series (*Philosophes de tous les temps,* Paris: Seghers).

3.1. *The axes of language*

3.1.1. *The basic concepts of the theory of the two axes.*
When we speak, we carry out two acts. We make a selection from a pregiven stock of linguistic units and combine them into more complex units. Every element of discourse is thus extended along two axes. It occurs in *combination* with other units, in which it finds its *context*, while also providing the context for the units of which it is itself composed. On the other hand, every unit of a message represents a *selection* from a stock of units which can be *substituted* for it without rendering the message meaningless or wrong. On the first axis, designated as *syntagmatic* by Saussure, we have for instance the sentence:

My — father — is reading —   the —   news.

On the second axis, for which Hjelmslev's designation *paradigmatic* has been adopted, we choose each word from a series of words of the same kind and decide on one variant of several possible messages:

My — father — is reading —   the —   news.
His — uncle — is skimming — that —   newspaper.
That — man   — is studying — a   —   page.

The two activities, selection and combination, can be assigned to the two dominant forms of association in traditional psychology and to the two most common figures of speech in poetics. The units on the axis of selection stand in a relation of *similarity* to each other and thus prove to have an aspect in common with the figure of speech, the *metaphor*. A metaphor results from transferring the designation of one thing to another which is connected with the first through similarity ("He is a star" for "He is a superb player"). The elements of combination are related by *contiguity* and can be compared with *metonymy*. In metonymy the transferral of the name for one thing to another rests on some kind of contact between the two things ("I'll drink a glass" for "I'll drink wine"). This description of the speech act yields two columns of polar determinants:

Paradigmatic Axis	*Syntagmatic Axis*
selection	combination
substitution	contexture
similarity	contiguity
metaphor	metonymy

3.1.2. *Its evolution: Kruszewski, Saussure, Jakobson.* The Polish scholar M. Kruszewski (1884ff.:172) was the first to formulate the theory of the two axes.

> Every word is linked by two kinds of bonds: namely, 1. by innumerable bonds of similarity with words related to it in sound, structure, and meaning; and 2. by equally numerous bonds of contiguity with its diverse companions in different modes of discourse. A word is always a member of certain families or systems of words and at the same time a member of specific syntactic sequences of words.

Saussure (1916:177ff.) adopted, modified, and further developed this two-fold division of the units of language.

Saussure's most important modification consists in his restricting the associative characterization almost exclusively to the paradigmatic axis. One may assume that this modification was a consequence of the insight that a mere linear sequence of units does not produce a meaningful syntagma (e.g., "of on goes men we"). The contiguity of linguistic elements is not enough to constitute a meaningful syntagma. This demands an ordered syntactic relationship. Saussure's reserve in adopting a description of the syntagmatic axis in terms of the theory of association reveals a drawback of that theory with regard to the paradigmatic axis as well. Contrary to contiguity for the syntagmatic axis, similarity in the literal sense of the word is constitutive for the paradigmatic relation, although only in the simplest forms of paradigmatic substitution. Substitutions on a higher level involving the syntactic structure of a sentence, i.e., transformations, are subject to grammatical laws as well, which cannot be reduced to simple relations of association.

Kruszewski and Saussure both stress the creative aspect of associative, paradigmatic relations. Once an English native speaker has learned the derivation *to paint—the painter*, he can easily understand and even himself derive the substantive *the designer* from the verb *to design* on the basis of the associative similarity of the two verbs *to paint* and *to design,* although he may never have heard the noun *designer* before. Only creativity by analogy was studied by Kruszewski and Saussure; it rests on a relation of similarity and consists of the extension of a rule. However, more important still is the transformational creativity preceding it, in our example the nominalization of the verb. The transformation of the sentence "He paints" into the sentence "He is a painter" demands a higher level of competence than the analogous formation *painter—designer.*

Human language is primarily differentiated from other sign systems, including "animal languages," by these trans-associative laws of combination and substitution. The advantage of viewing the two axes of language in terms of the theory of association lies above all—as will be shown in the following—in the possibility of its extension, i.e., its fruitful application to the phenomena of aphasia, poetry, and also nonlinguistic sign systems. The properties uncovered by this theory are those which connect language with other sign systems and not those which distinguish the former from the latter.

Saussure extended the system of the two axes by assigning antinomies basic to his linguistic theory to the axes and by characterizing the syntagmatic relation as a relation *in praesentia* and the paradigmatic relation as a relation *in absentia.* The combined units are actually present in a sequence. The paradigmatic groupings exist potentially in the memory of the speakers.

Paradigmatic Axis	*Syntagmatic Axis*
in absentia	*in praesentia*
langue (code)	*parole* (message)
synchrony (statics)	diachrony (dynamics)

Jakobson restricts the assignment of all three pairs of terms to the two axes. The first assignment coincides with Saussure's principle of linearity (2.4.2.2. above). Distinctive features on the phonological level and units of meaning on the semantic level can both, however, be simultaneously given *in praesentia* (Jakobson, 1939a:SW I 307).

Saussure himself qualified the second pair in his *Cours* (1916:14f. and 124f.). There are rigidly fixed combinations and above all general combinatorial rules which can be assigned only to the code. The code determines which combinations are compulsory, which optional, and which excluded. Combination is largely "prefabricated" (Jakobson, 1939a:SW I 306f.; 1956b:SW II 242), especially on the lowest levels of distinctive features (phonemes and morphemes) and in certain literary and historical genres (fairytales, poems, spoken formalities of greeting and congratulation, etc.).

The combination of sections of discourse is obviously a process that takes place through time. Selection, however, gives the impression of an instantaneous decision. In any case, the groupings on the paradigmatic axis appear as static and simultaneous occurrences. Therefore, the two axes were also coordinated with Saussure's paired concepts synchrony/ diachrony and static/dynamic. This arrangement does not prove consistently valid either (1939a:SW I 306). The code is not something that has been dropped ready-made into our laps. It must first of all be constituted and then subjected to constant modifications on the phylogenetic and ontogenetic levels. The distinction in a language between the phonemes /l/ and /r/ must be created or acquired. Initially the child pronounces *road* no differently from *load*. The linguistic change from Latin to French (e.g., from *amor* to *amour*) and from child to adult (the replacement of *papa* by *father*) affects the paradigmatic axis of selection and substitution.

The grammatical processes that are the concern of transformational grammar can also be assigned to the paradigmatic axis. Chomsky's grammar has, as we have seen, accomplished a systematic paradigmatic investigation of syntax. Jakobson (1972d:14), therefore, favors Bierwisch's approach (1966), which treats Chomsky's transformational grammar as a chapter in the history of structural linguistics.

The complex temporal considerations of the theory of the two axes in European structuralism become evident in comparison with the scheme which in American structuralism plays a similar, though somewhat less extensive, role and which coincides with that theory to a certain extent. Hockett (1954) distinguishes two major models of linguistic theories. The one, called *item and arrangement*, investigates linguistic forms in their linear distribution. According to this model, language consists of *simple* and *composite* forms. Simple forms occur as *immediate constituents* of composite forms. The other model, called *item and process*, explores the relations among forms as a developmental process. Such processes are, for instance, affixation (*occupy — preoccupy*), nominalization (*to occupy — occupation*), as well as predication, etc. Language in this model consists of *simple* and *derived* forms. The former occur as *underlying forms* which become *derived forms* through a process. Bloomfield and his followers are mentioned as proponents of the first model; Boas, Sapir, and Chomsky as proponents of the second.

One point in Hockett's conception is of particular interest for our problem. The syntagmatic axis appears in a static perspective, the paradigmatic axis in a dynamic one. The static approach to the syntagmatic axis can be explained by the dominant orientation of post-Bloomfieldian linguistics in the United States toward the analysis of an actually present corpus of linguistic units. By and large, the code of a language is reduced to the laws of arrangement of its individual *items.*

Jakobson's contribution to the theory of the two axes lies in his critical treatment of Saussure's version, in his assignment of the two figures of speech, metaphor and metonymy, to the two axes, and above all in his fruitful extension of their application, most profoundly to the phenomena of aphasia and poetry, but also to the different attitudes of speaker and listener to language, and in outline to diverse nonlinguistic sign systems.

3.1.3. *The two axes in aphasia and poetry.* Jakobson (several articles since 1955: see SW II 229ff.) distinguishes two main types of aphasia, depending on whether the paradigmatic axis of selection or the syntagmatic axis of combination is impaired. In the first case, he speaks of a "similarity disorder," in the second, of a "contiguity disorder." An aphasic suffering from a similarity disorder loses the ability to produce a meaningful substitution, the ability to use synonyms, metalinguistic circumlocutions, translations into other languages or other sign systems, and even the ability simply to repeat a word. The stimulus *champagne* does not elicit such answers as "I mean fizz" (colloquial synonym) or "You know, the sparkling white wine from France" (circumlocution) or "I said champagne" (pleonasm). Instead, he switches to a metonymic track with a response that has some kind of (temporal, spatial, or causal) connection with champagne. He might mention a hangover (temporal and causal relationship) or a bottle (spatial receptacle) or the foam (*pars pro toto*). Either he uses only the most general words or he uses expressions that are restricted to a specific concrete context. Instead of a "knife," he speaks of a "thing," or, depending on the situation, of a "breadknife," a "pencil sharpener," or, context interwoven, of a "knife and fork." Words with an inherent reference to the context he retains the longest, i.e., pronouns, adverbs, auxiliary verbs, etc. One of Jakobson's most striking examples for this type of aphasia (1966a:SW II 329f.) concerns a French patient, who is able to respond correctly to a particular situation with the answers *J'écris* ("I'm writing") and *Il écrit* ("He is writing"), but cannot say *Vous écrivez* ("You are writing") and *Elle écrit* ("She is writing"). *Je* and *il* are preverbal prefixes which can only be used in a context, while *vous* and *elle* are autonomous pronouns which can also occur without a verb. This kind of aphasic finds it hard to start a conversation. It is easier for him to continue the thread of a conversation once begun.

Other difficulties confront the aphasic suffering from a contiguity disorder. He is incapable of forming connected sentences. Relational words escape him. The more syntactically independent a word is, the better he can retain it. The result is a telegraphic style. Substantives dominate. These aphasics have lost the ability to compose and analyse a context. A word no longer serves as a constituent for a more complex unit. A compound word (*staircase*) will be correctly applied; its components are, however, no longer recognized or treated as such.

Jakobson (1964c:SW II 289ff.) did not stop here with his linguistic analysis of aphasia. He proceeded to examine the six types distinguished by the leading Russian neurologist and specialist on aphasia, A. R. Luria, in terms of the possibility of describing and explicating them in specifically linguistic categories, especially with respect to the two axes of language. The analysis of the first two types, in particular, is of general linguistic significance. Sensory and motor aphasia, as they are called in classical research, have to do with the ability to encode and decode linguistic messages. The encoding disorder manifests itself in combinatorial difficulties, known as agrammatism. A decoding impairment is revealed by phenomena to which Jakobson applied the term similarity disorder, i.e., the inability to execute metalinguistic operations and the depletion of nouns acting as subjects, with which selection usually begins in the formation of sentences.

The encoding disorder primarily affects the context, while autonomous elements remain largely intact. A decoding disorder takes the opposite course: autonomous elements dissolve, context-dependent elements are retained. In explanation of these findings, Jakobson points to the difference between the constitution of the encoding and decoding processes.

Encoding starts with the selection of constituents which are to be combined and integrated into a context. Selection is the antecedent, whereas building up the context is the consequent or the aim of the encoder. For the decoder this order is inverted. First the decoder is faced with the context, second, he must detect its constituents; combination is the antecedent, selection is the consequent, that is, the ultimate aim of the decoding process. The encoder begins with an analytic operation which is followed by synthesis; the decoder receives the synthesized data and proceeds to their analysis. In aphasic disorders the consequent is impaired, while the antecedent remains intact; combination, therefore, is deficient in the encoding types of aphasia, and selection in the decoding types. (1964c:SW II 296)

The comparison of the structure and the aphasic disorder of both processes yields a chiasmic picture (ibid.).

Encoding   *Decoding*
intact − constituents⟍ ⟋context − *antecedent*
impaired − context⟋ ⟍constituents − *consequent*

In poetics, from the late fifties on, Jakobson supplements the original phenomenological definition—according to which the essence of poetry lies in the set towards the message as such—with a basically structural definition. "The poetic function projects the principle of equivalence from the axis of selection into the axis of combination" (1960b:358). A poetic sequence is characterized on all levels of language by the reiteration of the same and similar elements (alliteration, rhyme, homonymy, synonymy) and by their contrastive variations (rhythm, antonymy, negative parallelism). In the case of contrast, the antecedent link of the combination is repeated in an implicit (i.e., negative) manner.

Tabák da bánja   "Tobacco and bathhouse
kabák da bába—   pub and female—
odná zabáva.   the only fun."
                                                    (1970a:108)

In this Russian proverb, the words have been chosen and combined in such a way that three lines with an even rhythm ensue. The arrangement of the four partial pleasures yields a chiasmic opposition between the two direct names (tobacco and female) and the two metonymical, local names (bathhouse and pub). For the sake of information alone, it would suffice to list at random the four pleasures. Poetry, however, is able to select among phonic and rhythmic equivalences and semantic differences of names. Thus the closed and rounded development of the thought is also expressed in its external shape.

In general, lyric poetry can be characterized as metaphorical and epic poetry as metonymic, not only because the former operates primarily with similarity and the latter with contiguity, but also because the lyric poet endeavors to present himself as the speaker, whereas the epic poet assumes the role of someone who has learned his stories by hearsay. Thus, on the literary level, we are once more confronted with the affinity between encoding and similarity on the one hand, and between decoding and contiguity on the other (1964c:SW II 297).

However, as shown by the contrast between Majakovskij and Pasternak, we also encounter within poetry and prose different styles dominated by one of the two principles of association. Romanticism and symbolism are obviously metaphorical, while realism with its predilection for synecdochic details and its meticulous situational descriptions is metonymic. Instead of speaking of the hero himself, the realistic novel covers page after page with a description of his clothes or his hotel room.

Of all the literary research in which Jakobson's explication of the theory of the two axes has been applied, we mention here only the studies on Proust by G. Genette (1970) and J. Risset (1971). With cogent examples they illustrate the curiously interwoven fabric of metaphorical and metonymic relations in poetic language. Proust's metaphors frequently rest on metonymic relations of contiguity. In the country a church steeple appears as an ear of grain, at the seaside as a fish, at breakfast as a croissant, at twilight as a pillow, etc.

3.1.4. *The general semiotic import of the theory of the two axes.* The bipolar typology can be extended beyond language and literature to other sign systems, to other cultural manifestations, in fact even to human behavior in general (1956b:SW II 256ff.). In painting, cubism with its dissection of an object into its aspects appears as a metonymic art; surrealism with its metamorphoses as a metaphorical art. The film operates with various angles, snapshots, and camera movements, and then submits all the stills to a montage. It is, thus, primarily a metonymic art. However, unmistakably metaphorical works may figure on this broadly metonymic background as well. Jakobson mentions films by Chaplin and Eisenstein and also Japanese films. In fact Japanese culture is molded by pronounced metaphorical strains (1967:158f.).

In ethnology, Jakobson sees an opportunity for the application of his dichotomy to Frazer's distinction between imitative and contagious magic, and in psychoanalysis, to the different mechanisms of the unconscious. Identification and symbolism would be assigned to metaphorical operations and displacement and condensation to metonymic operations (1956b:SW II 258).

Next to the phonological theory of the distinctive features, the concept of the two axes has perhaps become the most famous and successful chapter of Jakobson's linguistics. Almost unanimously, critics acclaimed his essay of 1956 for the aesthetic fascination and stimulating, broad-minded outlook of its conception of language. Some linguists did voice a certain scepticism regarding its empirical exploitability. Chomsky (1957b:242), for example, found it "suggestive and insightful, though still far from conclusive" (similarly Joos, 1957). Others expressed more optimism in their prognosis (for example, Greenberg, 1959); and indeed empirical confirmation was not long in coming. Luria (1973:62) wrote in a survey on the two basic kinds of aphasic disorders, "We can only conclude how correct R. Jakobson was, who was the first scholar to mention this basic dissociation in aphasics." The dichotomy has enjoyed such great popularity with French structuralists that one might be inclined to add the pair metaphor/metonymy to the paired terms *signans/signatum* and synchrony/diachrony which have been proposed as the criteria for structuralism by Barthes (1963:213f., cited above 2.5.).

Barthes himself (1964:63) applies it to clothing, food, furniture, and architecture. In fact, Saussure (1916:124) had already called upon architecture in order to illustrate the two linguistic axes. We can examine the column of a Greek temple either in terms of its constituents and of the other pieces of the building or in relation to its style. The spatial division corresponds to the syntagmatic and the stylistic division to the paradigmatic order.

Syntagmatic Axis	*Paradigmatic Axis*
base	Doric
shaft	Ionic
capital	Corinthian
architrave	mixed

In the same manner one can in clothing make a distinction between all the articles of a suit and all the variations in fashion of one particular article for a certain part of the body. The paradigmatic variation of single articles indicates the significance of the clothing, in other words, the role and status of the wearer. In clothing there is also a parallel to the linguistic "zero sign," which can be most conspicuous, for example, when someone turns up at a particular occasion without a head covering or a tie.

Syntagmatic Axis	*Paradigmatic Axis*
hat	hat
shirt	cap
tie	hood
jacket	helmet
trousers	cowl
shoes	turban

Finally, the menu at a restaurant may also be read as a syntagmatic sequence and as a paradigmatic choice of courses and ingredients. The "Choice of Dinners," shown below, was offered at the restaurant *Zur Münz* in Berne on May 19, 1974. It clearly illustrates this two-fold arrangement in the layout. The successive courses are connected to each other by three stars and the alternatives for each course by *or*.

CHOICE OF DINNERS

Orange juice   *or*   Consommé Monte-Carlo

Crème Montespan

* * *

Asparagus with   *or*   Northern surprise
hollandaise sauce

* * *

Fried chicken   *or*   Lamb chops with bacon
Cambacérès

* * *

Spring vegetables
Baked potatoes

* * *

Torte Pierre Carnot   *or*   Lemon sherbet Smirnoff

* * *

Sunday, May 19, 1974

In psychoanalysis, Lacan (1957:511) modified Jakobson's suggestion by pairing the two axes with the two principle mechanisms that Freud assigned to the unconscious. However, this coordination of the metaphorical axis with condensation and of the metonymical axis with displacement still leaves room for criticism (Holenstein, 1974a). There are not only metaphorical but also metonymical lines of condensation, for example, in the composite image, cited by Freud (1900:325), of a doctor and a horse (metaphor), which is moreover dressed in the nightshirt of the dreamer's father (metonymy). And one encounters obviously metaphorical displacements as well, when, for instance, a broken bone stands for a broken marriage in a dream or a joke (ibid., 409). Displacement has additionally the character of a substitution* (ibid., 339), while condensation can be described as a "merging and combining" (Freud, 1916/17:172).

Lévi-Strauss avails himself of the scheme of the two axes in his structuring of the varied achievements of the (savage) mind. Thus he (1962:204f.) characterizes the bird world as "a metaphorical human society" on the basis of the many parallels described with admiration in poetry and mythology. Dogs, on the other hand, as domestic animals, are considered a metonymical part of human society. In the procedure of naming, the relationship is reversed. Birds are usually given names taken from a limited class of names for human beings (Pierrot, Margot, Jacquot). The relation of bird names to human first names is that of a synecdochic or metonymical part to the whole. Dogs are frequently allotted names that now only occur on stage or in mythology (Azor, Fido, Diana), thus forming a parallel or metaphorical series in relation to the names people bear in everyday life.

Another illustration of the use of the two axes can be found in the different designations for colors and sounds (1964:22). Metonymical expressions prevail among colors, "as if a given yellow were inseparable from the visual perception of straw or lemon, or a given black from the burnt ivory used in its making." In sounds, metaphorical expressions dominate, e.g., "the clarinet, that is my beloved wife." We might add that we command no direct designations whatsoever for sound qualities, but only those which are primarily used for sense qualities.

Colors	*Sounds*	
snow white	light ⎫	(different kinds of
pitch black	high ⎬	visual perception)
blood red	full ⎭	

---

*"The outcome of the displacement may in one case be that one element is replaced (German original: *substituiert*) by another...." (Freud, 1900:339)

Colors	*Sounds*	
sky blue	sweet	(sense of taste)
grass green	soft	(sense of touch)

3.1.5. *The extension of the theory of the two axes.* The fruitfulness of the theory of the two axes lies not only in its many possible applications, but also in its potential for further extension (Holenstein, 1974a). This can proceed along two lines. To begin with, contrast, as in the traditional theory of association, can be treated as a genuine third form of association and not merely as a special form of similarity. The operations of both selection and combination presuppose an antecedent operation, the differentiation of signs, for which contrast functions as the base principle. As we have seen, contrast* frequently makes its appearance in linguistic differentiation in the overt form of opposition. With contrast treated in this way, it is possible not only to integrate opposition into a comprehensive concept of language oriented toward the classical theory of association, but also to assign the diverse phenomena of aphasia and poetry, which threaten to break out of the framework of the theory of the two axes, to their proper place in a comprehensive theory.

In the first phase of his studies on aphasia (1941), Jakobson focused on the reverse symmetry of the build-up of language in the child and its dissolution in the aphasic. The build-up of the phonological system obeys the law of the maximal contrast of sounds. In aphasic dissolution the most recently acquired contrasts are the first to be lost, while the optimal contrasts of the early phases of language acquisition manifest the most resistance. We can adjoin this phenomenon of aphasia as "contrast disorder" to the disorders of similarity and contiguity, to which Jakobson subsequently attributed central importance.

Another structural element of poetry of the same

---

*In linguistic literature, the term *contrast* is restricted to the difference between two consecutive units (1951:SW I 442; 1956a:SW I 465). We apply it broadly to every kind of difference that is constitutive of perception.

generality as projection of the principle of equivalence into the axis of combination is the accentuation of all latent contrasts that are constitutive of language. Russian formalism approached certain of these contrasts under the heading of estrangement. "We apprehend each new manifestation of the contemporary poetic language in its necessary relationship with three factors: existing poetic tradition, everyday language of the present time, and the developing poetic tendencies with which the given manifestation is confronted" (Jakobson, 1921a:18f.). On the syntagmatic axis, conspicuously prosodic elements are superimposed upon the opposition of distinctive elements of successive phonemes. These contrasts can be accentual (regular sequence of stressed and unstressed syllables), chronemic (long and short syllables), and tonemic (high and low syllables) in nature. In addition, we have the systematic exploitation of the latent tension between metrical and syntactic and between phonological and semantic units (2.3.2.3. above).

Jakobson's structural definition of poetry within the framework of the theory of the two axes can be extended as follows. Besides the projection of the principle of similarity from the axis of selection into that of combination, there also occurs in poetry a projection of the principle of contrast from its usual level of a latent prerequisite for linguistic relations into the level of an obvious, "palpable" form.

A second line of development opens up by distinguishing as two separate operations the mutual substitution of signs (commutation or transformation) and the substitution of signs for extralinguistic and extrasemiotic referents, and by then submitting this latter form of substitution to associative-theoretical consideration. In this respect, we follow the lead of the originator of the theory of the two axes, Kruszewski (1884ff.: 172, 307, 350). He, too, had included the relation of designation and meaning in his draft of a theory of language oriented toward the principles of similarity and contiguity. The discussion of this function of language has been reserved for section 3.2.4.

3.2. *The functions of language*

In his Moscow and early Prague period, Jakobson's point of departure for the functional exploration of language lay in the distinction between everyday language and poetry. He separated the communicative function of practical and emotive language, typified by the set toward the *signatum,* from the poetic function, which is manifested in the set toward the sign as such (1921a:31; CLP, 1929:14).

Later Jakobson combined his approach with the frequently cited organon model of Karl Bühler (1934:24ff.). Bühler developed his conception of the triadic instrumental character of language on the basis of the three fundaments of the speech situation, namely addresser, addressee, and things as the objects of discourse. Depending upon which of the three dominates, the discourse will manifest a primarily emotive, conative, or referential function. Jakobson expands this model by including the medium of language which takes on a life of its own in poetry and by distinguishing further factors of the speech event. He comes up with a total of six factors, each of which corresponds to a specific function of language.

> The *addresser* sends a *message* to the *addressee.* To be operative the message requires a *context* referred to ("referent" in another, somewhat ambiguous, nomenclature), seizable by the addressee, and either verbal or capable of being verbalized; a *code* fully, or at least partially common to the addresser and addressee (or in other words, to the encoder and decoder of the message); and, finally, a *contact,* a physical channel and psychological connection between the addresser and the addressee, enabling both of them to enter and stay in communication. (1960b:353)

The six factors with their corresponding functions yield the diagram in Figure 8.

The diversity of linguistic genres does not lie in the separate realization of the individual functions, but rather in their different hierarchical order. There is hardly a verbal message that fulfills only one single function. The dominant

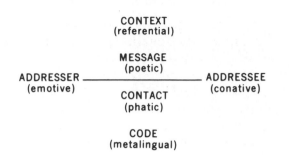

Figure 8*

*This diagram stems from a lecture held in 1956 (see 1975d). Compare Jakobson's two distinct diagrams of factors and functions in 1960b: 353 and 357.

function determines the structure of the message.

3.2.1. *The emotive function.* The emotive (this term was introduced by Marty) or expressive function centers on the personal attitude, status, and emotional state of the speaker. The addresser seeks to create an impression of a certain emotion, be it real or feigned. Interjections represent the purest specimens of the emotive stratum in language, although this stratum is, to a certain extent, inherent in every message. It indicates the attitude of the speaker towards the words spoken and can assert itself on the phonic, grammatical, and lexical levels. On the level of sounds, we have the distinctive features with their differentiating function in regard to the meaning of the discourse. In addition, we have emotive features, which convey information about the addresser. Both forms of phonic features are subject to the code of the language. They entertain a variable relationship with each other.

> The difference between [big] and the emphatic prolongation of the vowel [bi:g] is a conventional, coded linguistic feature like the difference between the short and long vowel in such Czech pairs as [vi] 'you' and [vi:] 'knows,' but in the latter pair the differential information is phonemic and in the former emotive. As long as we are interested in phonemic invariants, the English

/i/ and /i:/ appear to be mere variants of one and the same phoneme, but if we are concerned with emotive units, the relation between the invariant and the variants is reversed: length and shortness are invariants implemented by variable phonemes. (1960b:354)

Not only the emotional state of the addresser, his joy, fear, or irony, is revealed. With his choice of wording, he also displays his demands and his competence, primarily of course his linguistic competence. Every meaningful utterance indicates the implementation of acts of thinking. On the other hand, what is expressed need by no means be exclusively internal. Bodily behavior such as letting oneself fall wearily can be accompanied and accentuated by sounds.

3.2.2. *The conative function.* Orientation toward the addressee, the conative function, finds its purest grammatical manifestation in the vocative (noun) and in the imperative (verb). Both forms belong to the earliest acquisitions of child language. Their derivation by certain proponents of transformational grammar from declarative sentences, in which the referential function dominates, does not do justice to their uniqueness and genetic priority. In contradistinction to declarative sentences, imperatives are not liable to the test of truth, nor can they be converted into questions.

Magical incantations represent a special form of the conative function. They are not necessarily directed toward a living and present "second person," but rather toward an inanimate and absent "third person." "May this sty dry up, *tfu, tfu, tfu, tfu*" (Lithuanian spell, quoted ibid., 355).

3.2.3. *The phatic function.* In speaking of the phatic function, Jakobson adopts Malinowski's term to designate those linguistic messages whose primary purpose lies in establishing, prolonging, checking out, confirming, or discontinuing the communication. The phatic function is the first to be acquired and successfully employed by the child.

Dr. Niederland asked why, if the phatic function served the purpose of continuing contact with the mother, the infant's vocalization ceased when the mother was present. As with a parakeet who stops talking when children try to set up a dialogue with it (to their great frustration), the infant's purpose, Dr. Jakobson pointed out, that of establishing contact, has already been achieved when the mother is present and continues without the need for further vocalization. (1964d:4)

Many adult conversations, as well, have no other function than to prolong communication. Examples of a communication involving technical means are checking ("testing, one, two") or simple noises ("hum-hum!"). Their sole purpose is to make sure that a telephone or loudspeaker is working (1960b:355).

The performative function of many linguistic utterances, which has been thrust into the foreground by ordinary language philosophy, can for the most part be assigned to the functions listed so far, depending on whether the utterance is mainly concerned with the attitude of the first person ("I promise you," "I accept that gift"), the second person ("I order you"), or the contact between the persons ("I love you").

3.2.4. *The referential function.* The referential or cognitive function dominates ordinary discourse. We designate objects and bestow them with meaning.

In clarifying reference, Jakobson decidedly rejects the Saussurian principle of arbitrariness. Citing Boas and Benveniste, he (1944:SW II 482; 1962a:SW I 653) extends Saussure's own attenuation of this principle through recognition of relative motivation based on the relations of signs to each other. A language may at most be arbitrary only "from the point of view of another language" (Boas). Within a given language, signs and categories of signs are constituted along clear-cut lines. Saussure examined only the line of similarity of semantic components ("nineteen," "twenty-nine," "thirty-nine," etc.), although it is but one among many and can be exploited still further than it has been by Saussure. In many languages certain phonological features appear only in certain grammatical forms, e.g., only in suffixes or in certain classes of suffixes. They can thus serve as indicators of these grammatical categories (1965b:SW II 353). Moreover, (optimal) contrast can be decisive for the origination of new signs (Holenstein, 1974a:117ff.). Also of relevance in this context are the universal laws of implication, upon which the hierarchical constitution of the phonological and grammatical systems is based.

The relations of similarity between *signans* and *signatum* are a more frequent and common phenomenon than Saussure admitted. Jakobson transcends traditional scholarship of these relations on the lexical level (onomatopoeia) by drawing attention to the iconic or, rather, diagrammatic correspondences between the morphological and syntactic forms of language and its referents. According to Peirce's theory of signs, upon which Jakobson builds in this connection, a diagram is a sign whose own constitution reflects the relational structure of the thing represented.

> Morphology is rich in examples of alternate signs which exhibit an equivalent relation between their signantia and signata. Thus, in various Indo-European languages, the positive, comparative, and superlative degrees of adjectives show a gradual increase in the number of phonemes, e.g., *high-higher-highest, altus-altior-altissimus.* In this way the signantia reflect the gradation gamut of the signata.
>
> There are languages where the plural forms are distinguished from the singular by an additional morpheme, whereas, according to Greenberg, there is no language in which this relation would be the reverse and, in contradistinction to the singular forms, the plural ones would be totally devoid of such an extra morpheme. The signans of the plural tends to echo the meaning of a numeral increment by an increased length of the form. (Jakobson, 1965b:SW II 352)

The combination of morphemes into words and words into syntactic groups displays a certain diagrammatic structure as well. The semantic contrast between subject and object is exposed in the word order of the most fundamental declarative sentences, just as the semantic contrast between roots as lexical morphemes and affixes as grammatical ones is expressed by their differing positions within a word.

Jakobson (ibid., 347) describes Peirce's triadic division of signs into icons, indices, and symbols in terms of the theory of association. The icon rests on a "factual similarity," the index on a "factual contiguity," and the symbol on an "imputed, learned contiguity" between *signans* and *signatum.* Of significance here is that this trichotomy is not a division of individual signs, but consists rather of three different modes of signs. Each sign owes its name to the preponderant component.

The index character dominates the shifters, whose reference changes with every situation of discourse. The most obvious examples are personal, possessive, and demonstrative pronouns, as well as verb tenses. Shifters differ from all other constituents of the code by virtue of their compulsory dependence on the given message. This situational and contextual dependence, however, does not mean that they are denied a general meaning, as frequently claimed in traditional language theory. *I* consistently means the addresser and *you* the addressee in the messages of which these pronouns are components (1957:SW II 132).

In his diagram of six linguistic factors, upon which the theory of functions is based, Jakobson uses the term *context* instead of *reference* in view of the observation discussed above (2.3.2.4.) that there are no isolated referents without a context in which their designations are rooted. This context need not itself be linguistic in nature. But it is always semiotic in nature and basically capable of being verbalized. When we introduce a name for an object ("morning star"), we either depend on a name already familiar to us ("Venus") or on a potentially complicated paraphrase ("the planet that ..."), or we must use deictic signs (pointing with a finger, mechanical means of accentuation) and thus try to define it through its relation to these deictic signs. Every substitution of an object through a sign (signification) implies the substitution of a sign by another sign (commutation, transformation), and in this respect we can speak of a "closed universe of signs." It is possible in language to refer to something (factually) extralinguistic. But it is quite impossible to use language to refer to something absolutely extrasemiotic, to something that is not itself already semiotically staked. The universe of language may not be a closed system; the universe of signs certainly is. The naive distinction between language and (extralinguistic) world must give way to a more complex description. Jakobson's classification of three kinds of translation may be of assistance here, although we must remain aware that intersemiotic translation can proceed in both directions, from language to another system of signs and conversely.

> 1) Intralingual translation or *rewording* is an interpretation of verbal signs by means of other signs of the same language.
> 2) Interlingual translation or *translation proper* is an interpretation of verbal signs by means of some other language.
> 3) Intersemiotic translation or *transmutation* is an interpretation of verbal signs by means of signs of nonverbal sign systems. (1959a:SW II 261)

This "closed universe of signs" can only startle philosophers who are not familiar with the conception of the world in transcendental philosophy. Semiotic closedness is nothing but a reformulation of the inevitable enclosure of the world in our consciousness, as propounded by transcendental philosophy. With our ideas and concepts, we can never refer to anything that we have not already perceived, imagined, wished, thought, or otherwise been conscious of. Semiotics replaces these psychological and intentional terms by a term of its own, *designated,* by which it means "woven into a sign system."

3.2.5. *The metalinguistic function.* In the sphere of science, the term *object language* has come to be used for discourse about extralinguistic entities, and Tarski's term *metalanguage* for discourse about entities of a linguistic nature. Every science displays both kinds of language. On the level of object language, for example, astronomy deals with the stars and their properties. On the metalinguistic level, it is concerned with the basic principles and formulation of its own theory, absence of contradiction, the mathematical character of its laws, etc. The scientific ideal of a strict separation between the two levels stems from the discovery that ordinary speech uses expressions on both levels side by side and without discrimination, resulting in frequent conceptual muddles and logical antinomies.

In contrast to the prevalent criticism of use of metalinguistic elements in ordinary speech, Jakobson emphasizes their positive function in the acquisition and use of language. Without metalinguistic explanations, no child would be able to acquire his language, nor could we paraphrase the meaning of new and foreign words (2.1.5. above).

The fundament of language corresponding to the metalinguistic function is the code. Jakobson prefers the term *code*, from the theory of communication, to Saussure's vague and ambiguous term *langue*. As in Saussure's antinomy of synchrony and diachrony, there are also at least three independent antinomies concealed in the antinomy *langue* 'language structure' and *parole* 'speech act' (1939a:SW I 284f.):

	langue	*parole*
(1)	linguistic norm	linguistic utterance
(2)	language as supraindividual, social endowment	language as individual, private property
(3)	the unifying, centripetal aspect of language	the individualizing, centrifugal aspect of language

In many cases these three antinomies are congruent, but certainly not always! An individual linguistic utterance, for instance, presupposes not only a social but also a lasting individual linguistic norm; the speaker more or less modifies the social linguistic norm and stamps it with his own particular requirements, preferences, habits, and prohibitions, which he categorically imposes upon himself in all his speech acts. Thus, the concept of the linguistic norm does not coincide with that of the supraindividual norm. On the other hand, choric utterances demonstrate that the concept of the linguistic utterance certainly does not have to coincide with that of the individual one. . . . Language as the individual property of the speaker, i.e., the individual linguistic norm, necessarily contains both centripetal and centrifugal drives, in other words, both communal and particular components. But as a social endowment as well, language always and inevitably fosters both of these drives, of which Saussure, by the way, was already aware: *la force unifiante,* on the one hand, and *l'esprit particulariste,* on the other. (ibid., 285)

In more recent writings, Jakobson deals mainly with the delineation of the third point listed above. The code is not a monolithic block. Saussure's model of *langue* as a static and uniform system gives way to a dynamic conception of a diversified and convertible code, a code capable of adapting to the different functions of language and the changing conditions of space and time (1974e:37f.). The code is also differently structured for speaker and listener. We have already indicated that for the speaker the paradigmatic operation of selection supplies the basis for the encoding process, while the listener engages the syntagmatic combination in decoding the message (3.1.3. above). The hierarchy of sound and meaning undergoes an inversion as well in the transition from speaker to listener.

Roughly, the encoding process goes from meaning to sound and from the lexicogrammatical to the phonological level, whereas the decoding process displays the opposite direction—from sound to meaning and from features to symbols. While a set (*Einstellung*) toward immediate constituents takes precedence in speech production, for speech perception the message is *first* a stochastic process. The probabilistic aspect of speech finds conspicuous expression in the approach of the listener to homonyms, whereas for the speaker homonymy does not exist. When saying /sʌn/, he knows beforehand whether "sun" or "son" is meant, while the listener depends on the conditional probabilities of the context.

For the receiver, the message presents many ambiguities which
were unequivocal for the sender. (1961a:SW II 575f.)

Not all references of language to language itself are
references of the message to the code. The message and the
code can each function both as object referred to (referent)
and as object used (sign). Depending on whether both
vehicles of communication are utilized and referred to at the
same time or function distinctly, Jakobson speaks of circularity or overlapping. Four possible relationships are distinguished (1957:SW II 130).

Type of Reference		*Sign*	*Referent*
(1)	circularity: M/M	message (referring to)	message
	C/C	code	code
(2)	overlapping: M/C	message	code
	C/M	code	message

(*M/M*). Quotations are messages concerning messages.
They occur as a message within a message. There are many
possible ways of quoting, such as direct and indirect speech
and different modes of reporting. In written language we
usually indicate direct speech with quotation marks. Certain
languages use a special morphological form to denote quoted
testimony. Thus in Tunica all statements based on hearsay
exhibit a "quotative postfix" (*-áni*).

(*C/C*). A proper name, "Dick," refers to every person
who bears this name. The circularity of the type C/C in
determining the meaning of proper names is as obvious as it is
inevitable. "The appellative 'pup' means a young dog,
'mongrel' means a dog of mixed breed, ... while 'Fido'
means nothing more than a dog whose name is 'Fido'"
(1957:SW II 131). The difference between proper names
("Fido") and appellatives ("pup," "mongrel") does not,
however, go so far as to endow only the latter with a general
meaning. Jakobson repudiates the thesis of logical semantics,
which assigns a proper name to one and only one referent
and denies all possibility of a broader meaning. "The context

indicates whether we speak about Napoleon in his infancy, at Austerlitz, in Moscow, in captivity, on his deathbed, or in posthumous legends, whereas his name in its general meaning encompasses all those stages of his life-span" (1959b:SW II 268). A person or a city can bear different names for different temporal segments and, we may add, for different roles: Byzantium — Constantinople — Istanbul. Constantinople is not merely the name of the city that was located on the Bosporus from the days of Constantine, who made it the capital city of the Roman Empire, until the Turkish Conquest. Constantinople is still the name of the same city today inasmuch as it is understood to be the seat of the ecumenical patriarch. Similarly, a woman scientist can still use her maiden name after she is married. Her husband's name marks her as wife and private person; her maiden name, under which she continues to publish, as scientist.

(*M/C*). We speak of metalinguistic use in the sphere of science only when the message refers to the code as discussed above. When we say "The pup is whimpering," the word *pup* designates a young dog, i.e., an extralinguistic object. However, when we say, "*Pup* means a young dog," or "*Pup* is a three-letter noun," then the word *pup* designates itself. It functions as an autonym.

(*C/M*). The meaning of shifters (3.2.4. above) is bound to the message. The general meaning of a shifter (*I, my, now*) cannot be defined without reference to the message.

3.2.6. *The poetic function.* Characteristic of the poetic function is the set toward the message as such, toward the linguistic medium in all its aspects and facets. In this set, language becomes conscious in its "self-valuation" (1921a:28), which promotes and cultivates the latent structures that pass unnoticed in the set of ordinary discourse toward the referent. In particular, the principle of equivalence, assigned primarily to the paradigmatic axis in ordinary speech, is projected into the syntagmatic axis.

It was through the field of poetry that Jakobson discovered and extracted the most important principles of structural linguistics: the autonomy of language, the structural character of language (the interdependence of the whole and the parts), the role of apperception (*Einstellung*), the interaction between sound and meaning and between prosodic (metrical) and grammatical structure, the two axes of language, the diversity of linguistic functions, etc.

The poetic and aesthetic function is not the sole and exclusive reserve of poetry. Rather, it is, in the art of words, the predominant and structurally determining factor. The other functions need not be absent in poetic texts. They merely play a subordinate role, just as in other linguistic genres, the poetic function is not absent, but only appears in a subordinate role (in political slogans, in advertising, in commemorative speeches, in child language, etc.). "The linguistic study of the poetic function must overstep the limits of poetry, and, on the other hand, the linguistic scrutiny of poetry cannot limit itself to the poetic function" (1960b:357).

Folklore occupies a special place within poetry (ibid., 369; 1966b:SW IV 637ff.). With their clear-cut, stereotyped, and crystallized forms, folkloric texts are eminently suited for the distillation of a structural analysis. Jakobson (1973a: 489) appeals to a similar structural conciseness as the reason for "the only restriction that I allowed myself in the choice of texts." This restriction concerns the length of poems. Relatively short texts "enable us up to the end of a poem to retain the vivid impression of its beginning, thus making us particularly sensitive and receptive to the whole poem, to the *totality* of its effect." Here again poetry points to a more general linguistic law. Language is not a Markov-chain, whose every link is determined exclusively by the immediately preceding links, according to statistical laws of probability. The subsequent parts of a discourse retrospectively affect the shape of the earlier parts (ibid., 494f.).

3.3. *The units of language*

3.3.1. *The descending scale of code dependence or the ascending scale of freedom.* The most obvious and least problematic arrangement for a handbook on language would seem to be the ascending series of increasingly comprehensive units: distinctive feature — phoneme — morpheme — word — phrase — sentence — utterance or text. But since this arrangement is not merely quantitative in nature, it erroneously appears to be less problematic. Each ascending unit is also qualitatively and structurally different from the preceding one. The code sets different limitations for each linguistic unit. Subjectively speaking, the different relations to the code correspond to the different degrees of freedom.

> In the combination of linguistic units there is an ascending scale of freedom. In the combination of distinctive features into phonemes, the freedom of the individual speaker is zero: the code has already established all the possibilities which may be utilized in the given language. Freedom to combine phonemes into words is circumscribed; it is limited to the marginal situation of word coinage. In forming sentences with words the speaker is less constrained. And finally, in the combination of sentences into utterances, the action of compulsory syntactical rules ceases, and the freedom of any individual speaker to create novel contexts increases substantially, although again the numerous stereotyped utterances are not to be overlooked. (1956b:SW II 242f.)

The smallest linguistic unit, distinctive features which in combination yield phonemes, do not independently convey positive meaning, nor do phonemes themselves. They serve only to differentiate meaning and cannot occur out of context. As far as their selection and combination are concerned they are entirely determined by the code.

> Neither such bundles as /p/ or /f/ nor such sequences of bundles as /pig/ or /fig/ are invented by the speaker who uses them. Neither can the distinctive feature stop *vs.* continuant nor the phoneme /p/ occur out of context. The stop feature appears in combination with certain other concurrent features, and the repertory of combinations of these features into phonemes such as /p/, /b/, /t/, /d/, /k/, /g/, etc. is limited by the code of the given language. The code sets limitations on the possible combinations

of the phoneme /p/ with other following and/or preceding phonemes; and only part of the permissible phoneme-sequences are actually utilized in the lexical stock of a given language. Even when other combinations of phonemes are theoretically possible, the speaker, as a rule, is only a word-user, not a word-coiner. (ibid., 242)

Morphemes are the smallest grammatical units of a linguistic sequence that are endowed with meaning. The manifold forms of affixes in particular exhibit a stereotyped structure and a strict code-dependence. The meaning of these morphemes is completely and utterly bound to the context. In the word *days,* the grammatical meaning of the suffix *-s* (plural) is bound to the lexical meaning of the radical *day*.

The word, seen from the bottom of the scale, is "the highest among the linguistic units compulsorily coded," (ibid., 251) and seen from above, it is the smallest independent element of an utterance that can be detached from its context (1949b:SW II 104). The manifold aspects of language are focused in the word, as can be seen from the fact that "not only linguistics but also sociology, anthropology, and logic deal with the word" (1965c:SW II 536). On the basis of such considerations, Jakobson adheres to the word as a concrete and real entity in spite of diverse borderline cases. Word coinage is normally viewed as an infringement of convention. Neologisms find acceptance only if they can be explained by translation into familiar words or by a sufficiently explicit context (1955:SW II 234).

Sentences are predetermined as regards their grammatical form, but there is considerable freedom in their lexical makeup. In conversation we expect a free and creative filling-in of syntactic patterns (nominal phrase - verbal phrase) with appropriate words. On the sentence level only matrices are still given in the code. From this formal point of view, the sentence is the most comprehensive construction consistently subjected to compulsory rules of organization (1964c:SW II 297, 302).

Only to a limited extent is the combination of sentences

into utterances subject to grammatical prescription. The rules involved here are no longer those of subordination, but rather those of coordination. Pronouns in particular and also word order to a certain extent have proven to depend on a context that goes beyond the limits of the sentence. Depending on the genre, there are also on the text level strict rules of composition, coded matrices in which only part of the context is freely variable. Seen formally, proverbs (1966b:SW IV 637ff.), myths, and fairytales are, for example, such rigidly coded texts. Dialogue represents a special kind of utterance consisting of an exchange of messages which also follows more or less prescribed patterns (1974e:34).

The hierarchy of linguistic units "is perhaps the most striking and intricate example of whole-part relations" (1962e:SW II 283). The declaration of one of these units as the absolute base entity upon which all linguistics builds ignores this whole-part relation so characteristic of language. A linguistic unit can be identified only in terms of its two-fold dependence upon the elements of which it is constituted and upon the larger context into which it is integrated.

Significantly, Jakobson treats the hierarchical arrangement of linguistic units mainly in his studies on aphasia. The varied dependence of the different units on the code comes to the fore in aphasia. The mastery of certain rules of selection and combination is lost. These rules can either no longer be handled or are used in violation of the code. Thus, in one type of aphasia, called semantic aphasia by Luria, the different coding of morphological and syntactic units is no longer respected. Aphasics of this kind are conspicuous for their neologisms. They treat the formal patterns of word building the way an average speaker treats the formal patterns of sentence building. They apply them to words at random. Children, too, do not relinquish their freedom in building words until they have reached a certain stage of language development—to compensate, as it were, for the freedom they have attained in building sentences (see 1964c:SW II 302).

One of the most remarkable demonstrations for the "reality" of the hierarchy of linguistic units is the suffix -*s* in English. It occurs in three places—in the plural, the genitive, and the third person singular of the verb. Empirical investigations have shown that the child first uses the plural -*s,* then the possessive -*s* of the genitive, and lastly the -*s* of the third person singular. The sequence of loss in aphasia is the exact reverse. This hierarchy can be explained only in terms of the respective linguistic unit that is impaired. Language is built up from the simple to the complex and breaks down in the opposite direction, from the complex to the simple.

> In the efferent aphasiacs whom Goodglass and Hunt [1958] tested, the break-down of three phonemically identical desinences—*z* with its automatic alternants *iz* and *s*—presents a significant hierarchy, and a very clear principle accounts for the order of their dissolution. The higher the grammatical construction, the more imminent is its disintegration. The first to be affected is the clause, and, therefore, the third person singular verbal ending which signals the subject-predicate relation (for example *John dreams*) is the least viable. The possessive ending (*John's dream*), which signals a relationship within a phrase, is somewhat more resistant. The word is the last of the three constructions affected; hence the plural nominal ending (*dreams*), which depends neither on the clause nor on the phrase, is the least impaired. (1964c:SW II 295)

3.3.2. *Language and chess.* Language has often been compared with chess. However, in its multileveled and hierarchically ordered dependence on the code, human language differs significantly from the one-dimensionally structured game of chess. The rules of chess can be said to correspond to the syntactic rules of language. A chess move either complies with the rules (it is right) or infringes upon them (it is useless). But beyond that it can, like performative speech utterances, only be judged felicitous or infelicitous (as regards the goal of the action), but not true or false, as in the case of declarative sentences. Chess not only lacks a superstructure which allows the question of truth, but also—as Jakobson has emphasized repeatedly—a substructure corresponding to phonology.

A standard game of chess consists of figures whose metaphorical shape and designation represent the hierarchical value of the rule connected with the figure. A certain number of differently shaped figures suffices. There is only one condition: the pieces must differ from each other. How they differ from each other is not prescribed; this is not part of the rules of the game. The rules of the "language game," on the other hand, do apply to the makeup of linguistic signs and to the way in which they differ from each other materially. The replacement of a lost chess piece by another does not in itself belong to the game, while the replacement of one "speech figure" by another certainly does belong to the rules of the language game. Word coinage and substitute expressions borrowed from other languages are automatically subjected to the phonological rules of the language in question (1956a:SW I 465f.).

> The traditional comparison of languages with chess must not be overrated. By mutual agreement chess players may substitute any object whatever for a mislaid chessman, whereas no constituents of a linguistic system can be arbitrarily replaced, and the choice of a substitute is far from being substantially indifferent. Not only the rules of the game, but also the rules of substitution govern the structure of language, since its constituents are bound by inalterable laws of implication and incompatibility. (1958b:SW I 531)

In ordinary speech with its orientation towards the communication of sense and truth, the semantic and logical rules of compatibility of the combined units predominate. But "natural" language also contains language games, in which syntactic, morphological, and phonological rules take precedence over semantic and logical rules.

In children's rhymes one often encounters sentences with semantically senseless, but syntactically correct constructions, as well as word formations with a meaningless radical but with affixes that clearly indicate a noun, a verb, or an adverb (e.g., "the desters distered dosterly"). Besides these familiar constructs, one also finds linguistic formations in which there is a reduction to a phonological structure. As in children's rhymes, the impression given is not of senselessness, but rather of a "suprarational" formulation. The phenomena of glossalalia belong to this category. Jakobson would not have remained true to the motto he borrowed from Terence, had he not dealt with this strange linguistic phenomenon.

Two characteristics typify glossalalia: the use of unusual phonemes and clusters of phonemes (e.g., *f* and *ndr* in the charms of Russian sectaries), which lends the impression of "speaking in foreign languages," and highly rigorous and transparent rules of phonological composition.

> Ivan Čurkin taught a worshipper to say while whirling: *Kindra fendra kiraveca.* An acquaintance with the rudiments of phonetics was sufficient to sight the rigorous selectiveness and recurrence of the sounds used and to detect that all four odd syllables of this sequence contained a front vowel while the vowel of all four even syllables was an apparently unstressed *a.* All three internal *a* of this formula, which fulfill the second syllable of its three members, were introduced by *r,* and the first two *ra* were preceded by one and the same cluster *nd.* Of the four odd front vowels, the first and third were *i* with an antecedent *k,* while the second and fourth were *e* with a foregoing labial fricative: first *fe,* then *ve.* (1966b:SW IV 641)

3.3.3. *Phonology.* Jakobson's most important linguistic work has focused on the smallest units of language—the morpheme, the phoneme, and their distinctive features. His findings have been discussed in detail in the preceding chapters. Since phonology has, to a certain extent, become the model science of structuralism, we shall briefly review Jakobson's most significant methodological contributions to this discipline. They can be divided into three sections: (1) the definition and elucidation of the phoneme concept; (2) the structural and functional description and explication of the build-up, modification, and break-down of the phonological system;

(3) the theory of distinctive features.

3.3.3.1. *The definition of the phoneme.* After the great historical studies on language by the neogrammarians, another new era in the theory of speech sounds was ushered in after the First World War with the systematic investigation of the distinction between the physical, physiological, and psychological study of the entire material domain of sound matter, on the one hand, and the strictly linguistic exploration of the function of these sounds in language, on the other. The former has been termed *phonetics;* the latter, *phonology* and *phonemics* or *phonematics.* *

The Prague linguists were able to profit from the pioneering work of Baudouin de Courtenay, Saussure, and their students on this methodologically important distinction and the corresponding distinction between sound and phoneme (sound in view of its functional aspects). The initial findings of the cooperative efforts in Prague were first presented in the "Thèses" of 1929 and the "Projet de terminologie phonologique standardisée" of 1931 (CLP).

Following up these findings, Jakobson further elucidated the functional and structural aspects of the phoneme.

From a functional standpoint, the phoneme is a sound that has a differentiating value. Two sounds whose exchange in the same linguistic context results in a change of meaning represent two different phonemes. If the interchange of two sounds does not affect the meaning of a word, they are considered two (phonetic) variants of one and the same phoneme. By the term *phoneme* "we designate a set of those concurrent sound properties which are used in a given language to distinguish words of unlike meaning" (1932c:SW I 231). This *functional definition* can also be called a *semiotic definition.* A phoneme is determined by its semiotic

---

*For many years the term *phonology* was more common in Europe, and *phonemics* more common in the United States. When Jakobson uses both terms side by side, he applies *phonology* in a broad sense to the investigation of the entire range of manifold functions that speech sounds can have, whereas his use of *phonemics* is restricted to the designation of the central portion of phonology which is concerned with the meaning-differentiating function of speech sounds (1956a:SW I 467).

function. This is a specific form of designation which only the phoneme shares with the "letters" of the genetic code of chromosomes. As opposed to other signs, these two have no positive, constant, and general meaning. With this specific semiotic function, phonology as a model science of structuralism faces a limitation that should not be overlooked (1973a:499). "All phonemes designate nothing but mere OTHERNESS. This lack of individual designation separates the distinctive features, and their combinations into phonemes, from all other linguistic units" (1956a:SW I 470).

A further definition of the phoneme is, in Husserl's terminology, the *eidetic definition.* It is based on the universal and invariant character that is inherent to the various sound realizations and unites them in a phoneme. "The phoneme is not identical to the sound, nor is it external to the sound. It is, rather, necessarily present in the sound, it is inherent to the sound and superimposed: it is *the invariant in the variations*" (1939b:SW I 315).

What remains invariant is "a complex unit," that can be described as "a bundle of distinctive properties" (1939a:SW I 303). This *structural definition* in terms of the combination of features has displaced the older definition of the Prague Circle, which describes the phoneme as "a phonological unit which cannot be broken up into smaller and simpler units" (CLP, 1931b:311).

With this three-fold definition in functional, eidetic, and structural terms, Jakobson refutes the other proposed definitions, which all in some way separate the phoneme from concrete sounds, i.e., the imagined or intended sound from the actually uttered sound (the mentalist view), the element of the code from the elements of the message (the code-restricting view), the class of sounds from its specimens (the generic view), the fictional, abstract construct from the real, concrete units (the fictionalist view). The mentalist and code-restricted definitions overlook the fact that other features besides distinctive features can be intended and can belong to the code. The generic and fictionalist definitions do not do justice to the "ontological" status of the phoneme.

The phoneme is a complex of properties inherent to concrete sounds (1956a:SW I 471ff.).

3.3.3.2. *The build-up, modification, and break-down of sound systems.* The main theme of Jakobson's phonological work in the years around 1930 was, in addition to the definition of the phoneme, the systematic and functional character of sound change. With his findings, he succeeded in bridging Saussure's antinomy of synchrony and diachrony (2.1. above).

Toward the end of the thirties, the focus of Jakobson's interests shifted from the historical modification of the languages of the world to the build-up of individual phonemic systems in child language and their break-down in aphasic disturbances. Once more he succeeded in delineating the systematic character of these developments.

> ... in all parallels between child language (or aphasia) and the languages of the world, what is most conclusive is the identity of the structural laws which determines always and everywhere what does or will exist in the language of the individual and in the language of the society. In other words, the same hierarchy of values always underlies every increase and loss within any given phonological system. (1941:SW I 373)

Jakobson illustrates the first phases in the acquisition of the phonemic system in the form of recurring triangles whose vertical dimension is characterized by the compact/diffuse opposition and whose horizontal dimension is characterized by the grave/acute opposition. Vowels and consonants are here joined in a unified system. The primary and fundamental split occurs along the compact/diffuse axis. It consists of the contrast between the optimally open vowel /a/ and the optimally closed consonant /p/. The next stage is formed by the consonantal split between oral and nasal phonemes (/p/ − /m/). This split does not occur in the following figures. The competing split between labials and dentals (/p/ − /t/) takes its place since the dentals play a leading role in the subsequent acquisition of the consonantal system.

The primary triangle /a/ − /p/ − /t/ splits into two

further triangles—a vocalic and a consonantal—following the same pattern. The specifically phenomenal characteristic of vowels is their outspoken compactness (saturation). Accordingly, their first internalized and sometimes only split takes place along the compact/diffuse axis. Consonantal sounds are of a more diffuse or diluted nature ("sounds with no definite saturation" [Stumpf]). Since the contrast acute/grave gradually prevails as saturation decreases, it understandably forms the first and sometimes only consonantal axis. On the other hand, the vocalic split along the consonantal axis acute/grave (/i/ − /u/) is secondary. In the same manner, the consonantal split along the vocalic axis compact/diffuse (/k/ − /t/) does not occur until after the specific split into acute and grave consonants. Figure 9 illustrates the five

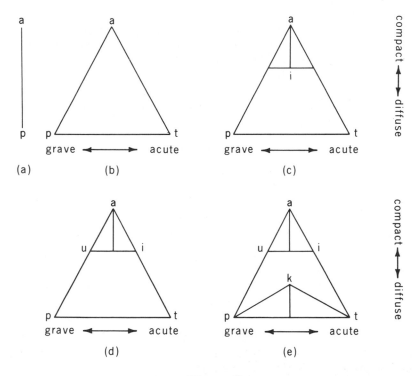

Figure 9

phases in the constitution of the three-fold phonological triangle (see 1956a:SW I 493).

The phonological triangle served Lévi-Strauss (1965; 1968:390ff.) as a prototype for his analysis of foodstuffs and ways of cooking them. Instead of the simple recurring axes compact/diffuse and grave/acute, the culinary triangle presents more complex, overlapping and, depending on the standpoint, reversible relations: nature/culture, unprocessed/ processed, presence vs. absence of mediation through air or water.*

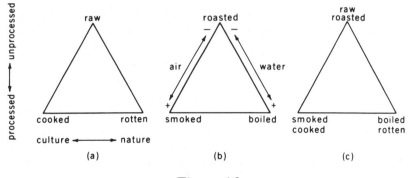

Figure 10

The first triangle, Figure 10(a), needs no comment. The second, 10(b), and its combination with the first 10(c) require elucidation. *Roasting* proceeds without the mediation of a cultural apparatus and without the mediation of air or water. The means and result of roasting belong to nature. *Boiling* is a process that reduces raw food to a state similar to rotting through the mediation of a cultural apparatus (receptacle) and water. The means belong to culture; the result to nature. *Smoking* is a variation of cooking which

*Jakobson (1965e) himself developed a triangle of "gustemes" in strict analogy to the phonological triangle. The compact pole of the sound system corresponds to the *plat de résistance* ("main course") as the peak of the gustatory system, and the base line grave/acute corresponds to the opposition bitter/sweet. Standard European and American dinners all follow the order bitter/compact/ sweet.

proceeds without the mediation of a cultural apparatus but with the mediation of air. The means belong to nature; the result to culture.

The culinary triangle demonstrates the possibilities and limitations of the application of methods extracted in phonology to other fields of data. The phonological triangle cannot be taken over as is. It only provides impetus for design of a model that allows for the specific structure of a different kind of subject matter. The phonological triangle illustrates how those elements whose unique function consists in differentiating meaning are constituted. The culinary triangle is a taxonomic model with the function of clarifying societal and cosmological structures. The arrangement of concrete sense data (foodstuffs, fauna, flora, etc.) serves as a model for the grasp of the less transparent arrangement underlying the data of society and the cosmos.

An immediate relative of the phonological triangle is the color triangle, which has been admirably elucidated by Dora Vallier (1975).* Vallier's sketches graphically demonstrate the synesthetic affinity between sounds and colors—an old theme of Jakobson's (1941:SW I 386ff.; 1949e; 1970c:SW II 689). The vocalic triangle corresponds to the chromatic triangle of light colors. Here the dominating axis is formed by the opposition of optimal and attenuated saturation. Corresponding to the consonantal triangle is the achromatic triangle of the neutral gray series with a dominating axis formed by the opposition of light and dark.

3.3.3.3. *The distinctive features.* During his last years at Brno, Jakobson had already laid the cornerstone for a new concept of phonology (1939a and e:SW I 272ff.), which he later systematically elaborated with his colleagues in the United States, mainly in the first decade after the Second World War (several papers: see SW I 418ff.; 1952a). Ac-

---

*For the formation of the color triangle and its comparison with the phonological triangle, Vallier proceeds from the phenomenological, perceptual experience of colors and not, as Berlin and Kay (1969:106)—in a questionable manner—from the physical nature of colors (amount of energy and frequency of light waves).

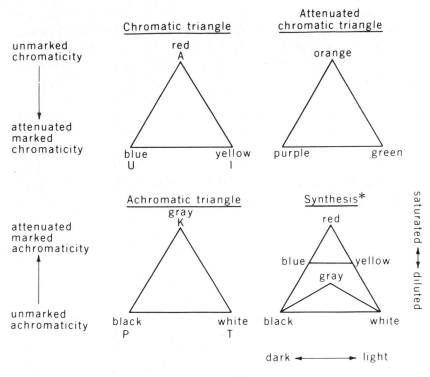

Figure 11

*Author's addition.

cording to the classical phonology of the Prague Circle, phonemes form pairs of correlations which are characterized by the presence vs. the absence of correlation marks. Thus, the basis for the thesis that phonemes do not represent the smallest linguistic units but are themselves divisible into still smaller units was provided by the Prague Circle, but had not been uniformly and systematically elaborated. With his systematic elaboration supported by a consistently binary definition and a subtilized physio- and psychoacoustic analysis of features, Jakobson surpassed his former colleagues

and transcended his own earlier conception of the phonological system.

The distinctive features fall into two large groups:
inherent and prosodic features. All phonemes, independent
of their position in the syllable, build upon the inherent
features. Prosodic features appear only in those phonemes
which form the culminant part of a syllable. Both groups of
features can be divided into three mutually corresponding
classes. Jakobson's theory states that no more than twelve
inherent oppositional features form the stock from which all
languages of the world make their individually restricted
selection for the constitution of their respective phonological
systems (1956a:SW I 479ff.; revised version 1968:SW I
738ff.). The three types of prosodic features, force, quantity,
and tone, correspond to the attributes of sensation—
voice-loudness, subjective duration, and voice-pitch. The
corresponding physical level is displayed by the varied shape
and extent of the intensity, time, and frequency of acoustic
waves. The three types of inherent features, sonority,
protensity, and tonality, show a close affinity with the three
types of prosodic features.

Phonological analysis of features, the division of complex units into matrices of positive and negative marks (2.5.2.
above), has become a prototype for analogous orderings of
semantic units (2.3.2.2. above) and of the most diverse
cultural phenomena (see Lévi-Strauss, 1968:85, etc.).

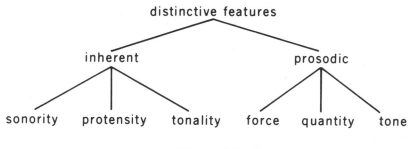

Figure 12

3.4. *The phases of the speech act*

Besides the sequence of ascending linguistic entities, there is an additional sequence consisting of the successive phases of the speech act. This, too, clearly involves a whole-part relation. The study of one phase implies the elucidation of its position in the speech act as a whole and the relationship of its structure to that of the other phases. In his most comprehensive enumeration, Jakobson names seven phases: "intention, innervation, gradual production, transmission, audition, perception, comprehension" (1962e:SW II 281).

The terminology here presents certain difficulties. What Jakobson has listed as "gradual production" is normally called (motor) articulation. The terms *acoustic* and *auditive* are not unequivocally defined. Acoustic is used to designate not only the phase of physical transmission (acoustic waves) but also the phase of psychic reception, especially in the older literature (see 1929a:SW I 23). In the "Thèses" of the Prague Circle (CLP, 1929:10), there is talk of "subjective acoustic-motor images." Today the term *psycho-acoustic* is often used to avoid confusion. In the following we also employ the term *audioperceptive* for this psychological stage of reception. What Jakobson designates as *audition* falls into two phases, a physiological and a neurological, i.e., reception through the ear and reception through the nervous system in the brain. The first phase can be called the otological phase of the speech act. We apply the term *audition* to all phases of sound reception. For the phase of comprehension connected with the perception of sound material, Jakobson also makes use of the term *apperception.* Taken from the older terminology of psychology and philosophy, this term refers to the intake and processing of sound material with respect to the grammatical and lexical structure of the language in question.

The first two phases of the speech event, intention and innervation, do not readily lend themselves to scientific investigation, and their structure still remains largely unexplored. This had also long been the fate of both the otological phase of reception and the neurological phase, transmission of vibrations registered by the ear membrane to the brain. However, remarkable advances have recently been achieved in just these two phases, following G. von Békésy's success in the thirties in defining vocalic distinctions such as back/front, rounded/unrounded, wide/narrow in terms of the mechanics of the ear. The characteristics of the sounds conveyed are coded in the brain in the form of the electrical activity of the nervous system. It is remarkable that complex linguistic sounds and sounds resembling language find a more stable response than simple and less "informative" sounds (1962f:XXVIIf.). Further researches have shown that the ears themselves already discriminate between linguistic and other sounds. Apparently the right ear perceives speech sounds more precisely, and the left ear, non-verbal sound stimuli. Even in this purely physiological phase, the specific system of signs to which a given sound belongs is decisive for reception (1964b:SW II 338). Thus, not only phenomenological but also neurological considerations justify distinguishing phonology from the general theory of sound.

Traditional psychology treated the starting point of every analysis of sound, namely auditive perception, as an epiphenomenon and one-sidedly built the entire theory of sound on the preceding stages. In the general psychology of sound, the physical level of acoustic waves served as the basis; in the particular psychology of speech sounds, the base was mostly formed by the physiological level of motor articulation. The advantage of each is obvious. Each provides "objective" entities or events to which the conventional methods of scientific research can be applied. Auditive perception as a "subjective" datum can only be approached phenomenologically.

The old theory of acoustics was not content with this advantage. It further sanctioned the privilege of its domain with two dogmatic principles—the principle of the priority of physical reality over psychological reality, and the principle of physico-psychological isomorphism. Guided by these principles, the old theory concluded that both characteristic properties of acoustic waves, amplitude and frequency, correspond to only two properties of perceived sounds, namely intensity (as the correlation of wave deviation) and pitch (as the correlation of the number of vibrations). The manifold phenomenological properties were reduced to variations of these two base properties, which were in turn construed as an immediate effect and faithful likeness of the physical properties.

Jakobson's approach to the problems presented here can be characterized as phenomenological in two respects. First, he recognizes the autonomy of the phenomenological level of sound perception and submits it to a genuine phenomenological analysis. In his contribution to the "Projet de phonologie standardisée" (CLP, 1931b:309f.), Jakobson divides phonetics into an organogenetic and a phenomenological part. *Organogenetic phonetics* treats the physiological and psychological formation of speech sounds. Its principal subject matter is "the motor representations of speech." *Phenomenological phonetics* treats "speech sounds as such, i.e., as the result of phonation, without consideration of the speech act." Its principal subject matter is "the acoustic [auditory] representations of speech."

The phenomenology of perception is characterized not only by the fact that it does not derive the structures of sense perception from the physical entities supposedly underlying them, but also by the fact that it explores these structures with a view to their meaning. It is thus distinguished from a purely positivistic phenomenalism which is content with defining the priority and autonomy of sense data as opposed to physical entities. Phenomenology insists on the interpenetration of sensuousness and meaning. The structure of sensory material is derived from its meaning (or more precisely, meaning-differentiating function). Perception and apperception can be separated only in the abstract.

Second, Jakobson's phenomenological attitude is reflected by the fact that he submits not only the phenomenological phase of sound perception but also the relationship between the various phases to a phenomenological analysis. Here again a structural and a functional component can be distinguished. The functional approach leads to the downfall of the hierarchy established by mechanistic, causal thinking. No longer do the physiological or physical events, which can be interpreted as the mechanical source of sound perception, receive priority, but rather auditory perception or the linguistic exploitability of the perceived sounds. Participants in a conversation are attuned to these sounds as linguistic values and not to their articulatory production or acoustic transmission (2.2.2.2. above).

The priority of auditory perception has been confirmed by genetic research into the acquisition of language and the learning of foreign languages. In ordinary conversation, articulation is bound to auditory feedback, and perception to motor feedback. The absence of such feedback can easily provoke insecurity and disturbances. However, this sensory-motor coordination is by no means a generalized phenomenon of linguistic perception.

Children are often incapable of keeping apart the articulation of words which they can, however, distinguish correctly in perception and in memory. These words remain homonyms for children in their own production of them as long as only the sensory or auditory level has been mastered, but not the motor level of the phonological distinction.

> One of the numerous examples is Passy's story of the little French girl who still used only diffuse consonants and therefore substituted *toton* both for *garçon* and for *cochon* but protested resolutely when in jest adults called the boy *cochon,* and the pig *garçon* or when they used baby talk and named the pig or the boy both *toton.* "It's not *toton* but *toton*," was the girl's angry reply. (1968:SW I 714)

Analogously, in the learning of a foreign language, passive comprehension usually precedes active mastery.

> Russians in the Caucasus often learn to understand one of the local languages and to discern by ear its sixty or seventy

consonants without being able to reproduce them or even grasp
the articulatory model of such frequent Caucasian phonemes as
the glottalized stops. . . . Many foreigners of diverse languages,
while discriminating and correctly identifying the interdentals in
English speech, fail to reproduce them, and substitute the native
/s/ or /t/ for the voiceless, and /z/ or /d/ for the voiced
interdental. (ibid.)

The structural comparison of the various phases leads to
a revision of the classical concept of psychophysical parallelism. The relationship of the diverse strata is not an
isomorphic one-to-one relationship. Rather, we are here
confronted with a transformation of subsystems, namely a
successive reduction of certain aspects resulting in an ongoing
exposition of oppositional, meaning-differentiating properties
from articulation through the various stages of transmission
to perception and apperception. The same acoustic wave can
be produced by different articulatory processes. A "dental"
sound can, with a certain amount of practice, also be
reproduced by someone who has lost all his teeth. The
tympanic membrane is unable to register all the frequencies
contained in a sound wave in the form of vibrations, etc.
The successive transformation of sounds from neurological
innervation via physiological articulation, physical transmission, and otological reception to psychological recognition is
not only a material transformation of sounds across various
"ontological" stages of sound realizations but also a structural transformation. The transformation in this case consists
of a one-sided reduction.

In the process of communication there is no single-valued
inference from a succeeding to a preceding stage. With each
successive stage, the selectivity increases; some data of an
antecedent stage are irrelevant for any subsequent stage, and each
item of the latter stage may be a function of several variables
from the former stage. The measurement of the vocal tract
permits an exact prediction of the sound wave, but one and the
same acoustical effect may be attained by altogether different
means. Similarly, the same attribute of an auditory sensation may
be the result of different physical stimuli. (1956a:SW I 488)

It is not the mechanic-causal dependence of later stages upon earlier ones that acts as ordering principle for Jakobson, but rather their orientation toward the function of language as a means of communication. The meaning-differentiating function of sounds on the level of perception serves to distinguish essential and inessential properties in the preceding stages (1951:SW I 438). "The closer we are in our investigation to the destination of the message, the more accurately can we gauge the information conveyed by the sound-chain. This determines the operational hierarchy of levels in their decreasing pertinence: perceptual, oral, acoustical, and motor" (1956a:SW I 488).

The methodological precision with which the coordination of the different phases of sound realization is clarified has made Jakobson's phonology a model for structural analysis of both individual systems and connections between systems, as urged by Tynjanov and Jakobson (1928d:81) in the structuralist manifesto. The coordination of systems, the "systems of systems," also has its structural laws, which must be investigated.

Structural analysis, moreover, is a wellspring of ideas in the productive ongoing development of the phenomenology of perception, which has been thrust into the center of philosophy by Husserl and Merleau-Ponty. The phenomenology of perception pursues the problem of realism and idealism and, more generally, the relation of nature and mind. Auditory perception with its cogent structure and the obvious connection of its diverse phases to the various ontological strata—physical, physiological, neurological, perceptual, and conceptual—may well be a far more appropriate candidate for the further explication of these questions than the visual perception to which Husserl restricted himself almost exclusively. In Merleau-Ponty's phenomenology of perception, the synesthetic experience plays an important role. There is no experience that is restricted to one single sense organ. Here, too, the perception of speech sounds is a promising candidate for the further investigation of this fundamental phenomenon.

The auditory perception of speech sounds can be related to the most varied natural and artificial accompanying phenomena. Synesthesia, which, in the narrow use of the word, consists of the connection between sound perceptions and "hallucinatory" visualizations of color, is only one such phenomenon (3.3.3.2. above). More important than this extraordinary example are the kinesthetic, articulatory co-experience of one's own spoken sounds and sounds heard from others, and labiolexy, the simultaneous perception of the externally visible movements of the speech organs of a co-present sender. Artificial forms of visualization are, on the one hand, written language and, on the other hand, radiographic images of articulation and spectrographic registration of acoustic waves. The development of spectrography was spurred on by the hope of finding "natural writing" for deaf-mutes. These hopes have been shattered by the excessive redundance of visible speech. Only its esthetic effect has come into play beyond the realm of scientific research. As a kind of graphic mobile, it accompanies spoken and musical performances. A fruitful evaluation of the additional phenomena accompanying all the phases of sound realization, such as labiolexy, or proceeding therefrom, such as writing, demands the same structural and functional procedure exemplified by Jakobson's work, especially that on the stages of physiological articulation, physical transmission, and psychological reception (Holenstein, 1974b).

3.5. *The interdisciplinary relations of linguistics*

The different phases of the language act and its manifold functions compel linguistics to cooperate with other disciplines. In view of the once prevalent tendency to reduce linguistics to psychology, Russian formalism and the early Prague structuralism strove to establish the autonomy of language and linguistics. Nevertheless, the main concern of the above-mentioned Manifesto of 1928 involves an "analysis of the correlation of the literary series and other historical series" and the relevant procedure. Interdisciplinary research took on larger and larger proportions in the years following the Second World War. Decades of praxis in interdisciplinary cooperation with its concomitant methodological insights finally culminated in Jakobson's broad survey, "Linguistics in Relation to Other Sciences," first published in 1970 (SW II 655ff.), with a second, expanded version, *Main Trends in the Science of Language,* published in 1974.

Not only the needs of linguistics motivated Jakobson to become a major exponent of interdisciplinary cooperation. The challenge came from other disciplines as well. Language, as a prime cultural phenomenon, is a subject of research in many different sciences. It is also the medium upon which every science depends in formulating theory. Thus, any critical science must needs be interested in the fruits of linguistics. In addition, pioneering work in methodology has made linguistics a model science and has placed this branch of knowledge among the leaders in the concert of sciences.

In his survey, Jakobson places the human sciences in concentric circles around linguistics. He bases the central position of linguistics on the highly regular and autonomous structure of language and on the fundamental role assigned to language in culture. There is no cultural phenomenon and no social behavior that does not in some way imply a communication. But language represents the most explicit form of communication. Moreover, all conceivable modes of communication contain language as a prerequisite or as an integral part, or can at least be translated into a linguistic form. In any case, it is easier to abstract language from other data of culture and to define it as a relatively autonomous structure than to undertake the reverse.

Jakobson divides the human sciences into three circles.

> Three integrated sciences encompass each other and present three gradually increasing degrees of generality: 1. Study in communication of verbal messages=linguistics; 2. Study in communication of any messages=semiotic (communication of verbal messages implied); 3. Study in communication=social anthropology jointly with economics (communication of messages implied). (1974e:36)

If one considers not only the human sciences but also biology, the science of life, a fourth circle can be added in the light of communication as the central problem. The forms of human communication then become a mere section, albeit a privileged one, of a much vaster field of studies, "ways and forms of communication used by manifold living things" (ibid., 44).

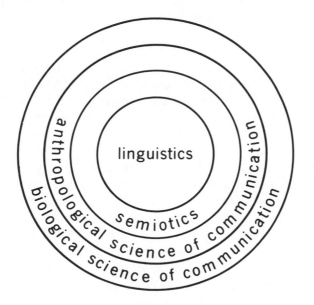

Figure 13

Semiotics, the general science of signs, forms the framework closest to linguistics, the science of verbal signs. The incorporation of linguistics in semiotics is to be understood as a conscious repudiation of its frequent treatment as a subdivision of psychology. As an underlying science, semiotics guarantees the autonomous character of linguistic structures.*

*R. Engler (1970:61ff.) has elaborated the theoretical significance of the incorporation of linguistics in semiology in Saussure's work. Striving to counteract the treatment of linguistics as a subfield of psychology and to throw

The affinities between classified objects and their relation to language provide the criteria for further sub-division. From this point of view, sign systems can be divided into three groups: (1) substitutes for spoken language, (2) transforms of natural language, (3) idiomorphic systems.

Substitutes for spoken language are writing, for example, and drummed and whistled "languages." The morse code exhibits a second order substitution. Its dots and dashes are a *signans* which stands for the ordinary alphabet as their *signatum.*

Transforms of natural language are the formalized languages of the sciences. The principal difference between natural and formalized languages lies in the context sensitivity of the former and the context freedom of the latter. Mathematics represents the most perfect formalized language. Natural language and mathematics serve as metalanguage for each other.

Jakobson designates those sign systems as idiomorphic which are only indirectly related to language, such as gesture and music. One must not, however, underestimate the significance of language for these systems as well. The acquisition of language affects all the other systems. A child's gestures are different before and after he acquires language.

The semiotic sciences are embedded in the wider circle of communication disciplines. Following Lévi-Strauss, Jakobson distinguishes three levels of social communication: (1) exchange of messages, (2) exchange of utilities (goods and services), (3) exchange of mates. These three levels are embraced by linguistics, or in a wider sense semiotics, economics, and social anthropology.

The affinity between linguistics and economics is a familiar theme. Money in particular appears as a sign system *sui generis.* In fact, it can even be transformed into purely verbal messages (checks).

---

light on the autonomy of language, Saussure, especially in his 1908/09 course, emphasizes the sociological component of language. In his 1910/11 course, semiology (semiotics) becomes the underlying theory and a rival of sociology, to which it had itself once (1901) been subordinated.

There is also a current linguistic criterion for the still disputed distinction between social anthropology and sociology, according to which the former investigates man as a talking being, and the latter as a writing being.

The relation of psychology to linguistics requires special treatment since psychology does not readily lend itself to inclusion in the three circles. There is, however, no dearth of points of contact and intersecting interests. Besides the interpersonal forms of communication, we must not overlook the intrapersonal forms, which occur between two phases of the same subject and whose principal function consists in the programmatic organization of future acts. Psychoanalysis also deals with a kind of inner language, whose gaps are filled by the therapeutic dialogue.

Within the realm of the biological sciences, two forms of "language" provoke a critical comparison with the verbal language of human beings: the so-called animal languages and the genetic code. We have already indicated the unusual degree of analogy between genetic and verbal information (2.2.4. above). Two explanations are proposed for this striking isomorphism: (1) The same function leads to the same structure. The genetic code and verbal language are the two memories of man; the genetic code transmits the molecular endowment and language the verbal legacy. (2) The molecular biological foundation of the verbal code also finds expression in the fact that its universal structure is modeled after that of the genetic code.

The behaviorist creed which holds that animal languages are distinguished from human speech only by degree long predominated. Jakobson is a decided proponent of the opposing thesis of a qualitative leap (1974e, 45ff.; 1975a). The uniqueness of human speech lies in (1) its creativity (in animal languages the entire corpus of messages is tantamount to their code); (2) its ability to handle abstractions, fictions, or, generally speaking, that which is not present in the situation of the speaker; (3) its hierarchical structure of constitutive elements as in (*a*) the dichotomy of distinctive and significative units and (*b*) the division of the grammatical system in words and sentences or coded units and coded matrices; (4) its use of propositions (affirmations and negations); (5) its reversible hierarchy of diverse functions.

Jakobson sets forth three universal phenomena unique to the human species: the manufacture of tools to build other tools; the rise of distinctive phonological elements that are without meaning in themselves and serve only to build meaningful units; the incest taboo as an indispensable precondition for wider social alliances. Common to all three is their auxiliary character; secondary tools are introduced to manufacture primary tools.

The qualitative divergence, however, does not preclude certain homologs between human and animal languages, and semiotics in general would suffer from their neglect. Both forms possess natures adaptive to their milieu, which can result in convergence as well as divergence in the expansion of communication systems. Additionally, both forms of communication contain inborn and learned aspects, so the opposition cannot be reduced to the simple dichotomy nature/culture.

Broadly speaking, linguistics and biology are related to each other through the teleological, self-regulative character of their systems. Physiology (articulation of sounds) and neurology (the neurological basis of the speech act and aphasic disturbances) overlap with linguistics.

Acoustics is the only branch of physics that shares its immediate subject matter with linguistics. Both fields of knowledge are becoming increasingly aware of common theoretical and methodological problems. Both are presently exploring the smallest discrete units of their respective systems.* Both are concerned with the problem of the interaction between the object under observation and the observer. It is this very interaction that brings into focus the aspects specific to each of these systems. In physics information moves irreversibly in *one* direction, from the object to the observer, whereas the linguist is faced with the

---

*In a lecture held in the early fifties, Jakobson introduced them as "The Elementary Quanta of Language" (1952b).

reversible process of intercommunication with those who convey the object of his research (2.2.2.4. above).

Jakobson views interdisciplinary research in the light of the two complementary principles of autonomy and integration, which also apply to the intralinguistic departments (2.4.2.3.). The uniqueness of every field of knowledge and the interdependence among the various sciences demand equal attention. An imbalance leads either to an isolationist bias, to a kind of fruitless apartheid or to an equally fatal heteronomy, a kind of colonialism in which the laws of one science are imposed on another science.

Jakobson's terminology reveals these ideas to be the fruit not only of sixty years of scientific endeavor, but also of a no less extensive and turbulent political experience.

BIOGRAPHY

1896	Born in Moscow
1905-1914	Studied at the Lazarev Institute of Oriental Languages in Moscow
1914-1918	Studied linguistics, science of literature, folklore, and psychology at Moscow University
1915	Co-founder and first president (until 1920) of the *Moskovskij lingvističeskij kružok* (Moscow Linguistic Circle)
1915-1916	Field studies in Russian dialectology and folklore
1916	Buslaev Prize for his study of the language of North Russian folk epics
1917	Studied at Petersburg University and participated in building up the "Society for the Study of Poetic Language" (OPOJAZ)
1918-1920	Research Associate for Russian Language and Literature at Moscow University
1920	Moved to Prague, studied at Charles University
1921-1923	First studies on linguistic poetics and metrics
1921-1928	Studies on Old Czech literature
1926	Co-founder and vice-president (until 1939) of the *Cercle*

	linguistique de Prague
1927	Lecture on Sound Change (repudiation of the Saussurian antinomy of synchrony and diachrony)
1928	Drafts for the foundations of structural linguistics and poetics as well as historical phonology
1928-1932	Period of the great programmatic congresses: First International Congress of Linguists (The Hague, 1928) First Congress of Slavic Philologists (Prague, 1929) International Phonological Meeting (Prague, 1930) First Congress of Phonetic Sciences (Amsterdam, 1932)
1933-1939	Professor of Russian Philology and, from 1937, of Old Czech Literature in Brno
1935	Morphological studies (theory of cases)
1938	First draft of a theory of distinctive phonological features, presented at the Third Congress of Phonetic Sciences in Ghent
1939	Fled to Denmark and Norway, Visiting Lecturer in Copenhagen and Oslo
1940	Fled to Sweden, Visiting Lecturer in Uppsala, studies on child language and aphasia
1941	Moved to the USA
1942-1946	Professor of General Linguistics and of Czechoslovak Studies at the *Ecole Libre des Hautes Etudes* in New York
1943	Co-founder and vice-president (until 1949) of the Linguistic Circle of New York
1943-1949	Visiting Professor of General Linguistics and, from 1946, Professor of Slavic Studies at Columbia University
1949-	Professor of Slavic Languages and Literatures, and since 1960, of General Linguistics at Harvard University; Emeritus, 1967
1957-	Institute Professor at M.I.T.
1966-1969	Interdisciplinary research at the Salk Institute for Biological Studies and at the Center for Cognitive Studies at Harvard University
1967-1974	Visiting Professor at the *Collège de France* and at the Universities of Yale, Princeton, Brown, Brandeis, Leuven (Belgium), and New York

BIBLIOGRAPHY

1. *WORKS BY JAKOBSON*

An overall view of Jakobson's publications up to 1971, including translations, is presented in: *Roman Jakobson, A Bibliography of His Writings,* The Hague: Mouton, 1971.

1.1. *Collected Works*

Mouton in The Hague is bringing out a seven-volume edition, *Selected Writings* (SW). Volumes I, II, and IV have already been published; volumes III, V, and VI are in preparation.

SW I   *Phonological Studies,* first edition, 1962; second, expanded edition, 1971.

SW II *Word and Language,* 1971.

SW III *Poetry of Grammar and Grammar of Poetry,* forthcoming.

SW IV *Slavic Epic Studies,* 1966.

SW V   *Verse and Its Masters,* forthcoming.

SW VI *Early Slavic Ways and Crossroads,* forthcoming.

In addition to the *Selected Writings* containing papers in English, French, German, Italian, and Russian, a number of larger and smaller volumes of collected papers have been published in English, Czech, French, German, Hungarian, Italian, Japanese, Portuguese, Serbian, Spanish, and Swedish. *Studies on Child Language and Aphasia,* The Hague: Mouton, 1971, has appeared in English.

Until publication of *Selected Writings* III, a French collection containing most of the important papers on poetics and the theory of literature is recommended: *Questions de poétique,* ed. T. Todorov, Paris: Seuil, 1973.

Early studies on the same theme are presented in an exemplary parallel text edition in two volumes with Russian (or Czech) and German: *Texte der russischen Formalisten,* vol. I, ed. J. Striedter; vol. II, ed. W. -D. Stempel; Munich: Fink, 1969 and 1972.

The periodicals in which Jakobson has published most frequently are *Travaux du Cercle linguistique de Prague,* before the Second World War, and the two American journals *Word* and *Language,* after the Second World War.

1.2. *Cited books, articles, interviews*

1919 "Futurisme." In *Questions de poétique.* Paris: Seuil, 1973, pp. 25-30.

1921a "Novejšaja russkaja poèzija/Die neueste russische Poesie." In *Texte der russischen Formalisten* II, edited by W. -D. Stempel. Munich: Fink, 1972, pp. 18-135. Partial English translation: "Modern Russian Poetry: Velimir Khlebnikov (Excerpts)." In *Major Soviet Writers,* edited by Edward J. Brown. London/New York: Oxford University Press, 1973, pp. 58-82.

1921b "On Realism in Art." In *Readings in Russian Poetics,* edited by Ladislav Mateika and Krystyna Pomorska. Cambridge, Mass.: M.I.T. Press, 1971, pp. 38-46.

1923 "Über den tschechischen Vers." *Postilla Bohemica* 8-10 (1974): 1-204. Cf. *O češskom stixe preimuščestvenno v sopostavlenii s russkim,* edited (with English translation of the preface to the 1926 Czech edition) by Thomas G. Winner. Providence: Brown University Press, 1969.

1928a "The Concept of the Sound Law and the Teleological Criterion." SW I 1-2.

1928b "Proposition au Premier congrès international de linguistes. Quelles sont les méthodes les mieux appropriées à un exposé complet et pratique de la phonologie d'une langue quelconque?" SW I 4-6.

1928c (with V. Mathesius, N. Trubetzkoy, Ch. Bally and A. Sechehaye). "Thèses." In *Actes du Premier congrès international de linguistes à la Haye du 10-15 avril 1928.* Leiden, 1930, pp. 85-86.

1928d (with J. Tynjanov). "Problems in the Study of Literature and Language." In *Readings in Russian Poetics,* edited by Ladislav Mateika and Krystyna Pomorska. Cambridge, Mass.: M.I.T. Press, 1971, pp. 79-81.

1929a "Remarques sur l'évolution phonologique du russe comparée à celle des autres langues slaves." SW I 7-116.

1929b (without title). SW II 711-712. Title by the editors of *Čin:* "Romantické všeslovanstvi—nová slávistika."

1929c (with P. Bogatyrev). "Die Folklore als eine besondere Form des Schaffens." SW IV 1-15.

1929d "Über die heutigen Voraussetzungen der russischen Slavistik." *Slavische Rundschau* 1: 629-646.

1929e "Dem Gedächtnis Jan Wiktor Porzezińskis." *Prager Presse,* March 17, 1929.

1930a "Jazykovye problemy y trudax T. G. Masarika." SW II 468-476.

1930b (with F. Slotty). "Die Sprachwissenschaft auf dem ersten Slavistenkongress in Prag vom 6.-13. Oktober 1929." *Indogermanisches Jahrbuch* 14: 384-391.

1931a "Principes de phonologie historique." SW I 202-220.

1931b "Der russische Frankreich-Mythus." *Slavische Rundschau* 3(1931): 636-642.

1932a "Musikwissenschaft und Linguistik." SW II 551-553.

1932b "Zur Struktur des russischen Verbums." SW II 3-15.

1932c "Phoneme and Phonology." SW I 231-233.

1933 "La scuola linguistica di Praga." SW II 539-546.

1934 "Co je poesie?/Was ist Poesie?" In *Texte der russischen Formalisten* II, edited by W. -D. Stempel. Munich: Fink, 1972, pp. 392-417.

1935a "Marginal Notes on the Prose of the Poet Pasternak." In *Pasternak*, edited by D. Davie and A. Livingstone. Corrected ed. Glasgow, 1971, pp. 135-151.

1935b "Formalisme russe, structuralisme tchèque" (Statements in the *Cercle linguistique de Prague*). *Change* 3 (1969): 59-60.

1936a "Die Arbeit der sogenannten 'Prager Schule.' " SW II 547-550.

1936b "Beitrag zur allgemeinen Kasuslehre: Gesamtbedeutungen der russischen Kasus." SW II 23-71.

1936c "Um den russischen Wortschatz." *Slavische Rundschau* 8:80-90.

1938 "Sur la théorie des affinités phonologiques." SW I 234-246.

1939a "Zur Struktur des Phonems." SW I 280-310.

1939b "Un manuel de phonologie générale." SW I 311-316.

1939c "Nikolay Sergeevič Trubetzkoy (16. April 1890—25. Juni 1938)." SW II 501-516.

1939d "Signe zéro." SW II 211-219.

1939e "Observations sur le classement phonologique des consonnes." SW I 272-279.

1941 "Kindersprache, Aphasie und allgemeine Lautgesetze." SW I 328-401. English translation: *Child Language, Aphasia, and Phonological Universals.* The Hague: Mouton, 1968.

1944 "Franz Boas' Approach to Language." SW II 477-488.

1949a "The Identification of Phonemic Entities." SW I 418-425.

1949b "The Phonemic and Grammatical Aspects of Language in their Interrelations." SW II 103-114.

1949c "Notes on General Linguistics: Its Present State and Crucial Problems." Mimeographed. New York, Rockefeller Foundation, 48pp.

1949d (with J. Lotz). "Notes on the French Phonemic Pattern." SW I 426-434.

1949e (with G. A. Reichard and E. Werth). "Language and Synesthesia." *Word* 5:224-233.

1951 "For the Correct Presentation of Phonemic Problems." SW I 435-442.

1952a (with C. G. M. Fant and M. Halle). *Preliminaries to Speech Analysis.* Cambridge, Mass.: M.I.T. Press.

1952b "The Elementary Quanta of Language" (Abstract). *The Journal of the Acoustical Society of America* 24:581.

1953a "Pattern in Linguistics." SW II 223-228.

1953b "Results of a Joint Conference of Anthropologists and Linguists." SW II 554-567.

1953c (with E. Colin Cherry and M. Halle). "Toward the Logical Description of Languages in their Phonemic Aspect." SW I 449-463.

1953d Statements on "The distinction between lexical and grammatical meanings" and "The interlingual aspect of linguistic changes." In *An Appraisal of Anthropology Today,* edited by Sol Tax et al. Chicago: University of Chicago Press, pp. 279-280 and 292-293. Cf. 1953a.

1955 "Aphasia as a Linguistic Topic." SW II 229-238.

1956a (with M. Halle). "Phonology and Phonetics." SW I 464-504. Partial revision 1968: "The Revised Version of the List of Inherent Features." SW I 738-742.

1956b "Two Aspects of Language and Two Types of Aphasic Disturbances." SW II 239-259.

1956c "Sergej Karcevskij: August 28, 1884–November 7, 1955." SW II 517-521.

1957 "Shifters, Verbal Categories, and the Russian Verb." SW II 130-147.

1958a "Morfologičeskie nabljudenija nad slavjanskim skloneniem." SW II 154-183. English summary 1962: "Morphological Inquiry into Slavic Declension." 179-181.

1958b "Typological Studies and their Contribution to Historical Comparative Linguistics." SW I 523-532.

1959a "On Linguistic Aspects of Translation." SW II 260-266.

1959b "Linguistic Glosses to Goldstein's Wortbegriff." SW II 266-271.

1959c "Boas' View of Grammatical Meaning." SW II 489-496.

1960a "The Kazan's School of Polish Linguistics and Its Place in the International Development of Phonology." SW II 394-428.

1960b "Closing Statement: Linguistics and Poetics." In *Style in Language,* edited by Thomas A. Sebeok. New York: Wiley, pp. 350-377.

1960c "The Gender Pattern of Russian." SW II 184-186.

1960d "Why 'Mama' and 'Papa'?" SW I 538-545.

1961a "Linguistics and Communication Theory." SW II 570-579.

1961b "Poetry of Grammar and Grammar of Poetry." *Lingua* 21 (1968):597-609.

1962a "Retrospect (1961)." SW I 629-658.

1962b "Zeichen und System der Sprache." SW II 272-279.

1962c "Anthony's Contribution to Linguistic Theory." SW II 285-288.

1962d (with C. Lévi-Strauss). "Charles Baudelaire's 'Les chats.'" In *Issues in Contemporary Literary Criticism,* edited by Gregory T. Polleta. Rev. trans. Boston: Little, Brown & Co., 1973, pp. 372-389.

1962e "Parts and Wholes in Language." SW II 280-284.

1962f "Concluding Remarks." In *Proceedings of the Fourth International Congress of Phonetic Sciences, Helsinki 1961.* The Hague: Mouton, pp. XXV-XXIX.

1963a "Implications of Language Universals." SW II 580-591.

1963b "Efforts toward a Means-Ends Model of Language in Interwar Continental Linguistics." SW II 522-526.

1964a "Visual and Auditory Signs." SW II 334-337.

1964b "On the Relation between Visual and Auditory Signs." SW II 338-344.

1964c "Toward a Linguistic Classification of Aphasic Impairments." SW II 289-306.

1964d "The Relevance of Linguistics for Psychoanalysis." In *Minutes of Study Group in Linguistics and Psychoanalysis,* edited by Dr. Rosen. The New York Psychoanalytic Institute, Meeting of May 11, 1964.

1965a "Znacenie Krusevskogo v razvitii nauki o jazyke." SW II 429-449. English summary: "Kruszewski's Part in the Development of Linguistic Science." SW II 449-450.

1965b "Quest for the Essence of Language." SW II 345-359.

1965c "An Example of Migratory Terms and Institutional Models." SW II 527-538.

1965d "Vers une science de l'art poétique." In *Théorie de la littérature. Textes de formalistes russes,* edited by T. Todorov. Paris: Seuil, pp. 9-13.

1965e "Szczupak po polsku." *Prace Polonistyczne* 20:132-141.

1966a "Linguistic Types of Aphasia." SW II 307-333.

1966b "Retrospect." SW IV 637-704.

1966c "Grammatical Parallelism and Its Russian Facet." *Language* 42:399-429.

1967 "Conversazione sul cinema con Roman Jakobson a cura di

Adriano Aprà e Luigi Faccini." *Cinema e Film* 2:157-162.

1968 "The Role of Phonic Elements." SW I 705-719.

1970a "Subliminal Verbal Patterning in Poetry." In *Studies in General and Oriental Linguistics,* presented to Shirô Hattori, edited by R. Jakobson and S. Kawamoto. Tokyo, pp. 302-308.

1970b "Prefatory Letter to Studies in Honor of Eli Fischer-Jørgensen." SW I 751-752.

1971a "The Drum Lines in Majakovskij's '150 000 000.' " *California Slavic Studies* 6:39-41.

1971b "Acknowledgements and Dedication." SW II V-VIII.

1972a "Verbal Communication." *Scientific American* 227/3:73-80. Expanded French version: "L'agencement de la communication verbale." *Essais de linguistique générale* II. Paris: Minuit, 1973, pp. 77-90.

1972b "The Editor Interviews Roman Jakobson." *Modern Occasions* 2/1:14-20.

1972c "Entretien de Roman Jakobson avec Jean Pierre Faye, Jean Paris et Jacques Roubaud." In *Hypothèses,* Collection *Change.* Paris: Seghers/Laffont, pp. 33-49.

1973a "Postscriptum." In *Questions de poétique,* edited by T. Todorov. Paris: Seuil, pp. 485-504.

1973b "Louvain Lectures." Cf. Marleen Van Ballaer, *Aspects of the Theories of Roman Jakobson.* Memoir, Katholieke Universiteit te Leuven, Fakulteit der Wijsbegeerte en Letteren, 1973. Mimeographed.

1974a *Form und Sinn. Sprachwissenschaftliche Betrachtungen,* Munich: Fink.

1974b "Life and Language." Review of *The Logic of Life: A History of Heredity,* by François Jacob. *Linguistics* 138:97-103.

1974c "Linguistic Contributions to the Pathology of Language." In *Lenguaje y Audicion: Normalidad y Patologia, Actas del II Congreso Panamericano de Audicion y Lenguaje y del I Congreso Peruano de Patologia del Lenguaje* (1973), edited by Artidoro Caceres Velasques. Lima, pp. 29-42.

1974d "Mark and Feature." In *World Papers in Phonetics: Festschrift for Dr. Onishi's Kiju,* Tokyo: Phonetic Society of Japan, 1974, pp. 37-39.

1974e *Main Trends in the Science of Language.* New York: Harper &

Row. Revised and expanded version of "Linguistics in Relation to Other Sciences" (1970), SW II 655-696, and "Retrospect" (1971), SW II 711-722.

1975a "Sur la spécificité du langage humain." *L'Arc* 60 (1975):3-8.

1975b "Glosses on the Medieval Insight into the Science of Language." In *Mélanges linguistiques offerts à Emile Benveniste,* edited by M. Dj. Moînfar. Société de linguistique de Paris, pp. 289-303.

1975c "Main Trends in the Science of Language" (Abstract of 1974e). *Studii si cercetări lingvistice* 26, no. 5.

1975d "Metalanguage as a Linguistic Problem." (Presidential address 1956). In *The Scientific Study of Language: Fifty Years of LSA, 1924-1973,* edited by Anwar S. Dil. Abbottabad, Pakistan: Linguistic Research Group of Pakistan.

1975e "Spatial Relationships in Slavic Adjectives." *Scritti in onore di Giuliano Bonfante.* Brescia: Paideia Editrice.

1975f *Coup d'oeil sur le développement de la sémiotique.* Studies in Semiotics. Vol. 3. Bloomington: Indiana University Publications.

2. *FESTSCHRIFTS AND SPECIAL ISSUES OF PERIODICALS IN JAKOBSON'S HONOR*

Romanu Jakobsonovi—Pozdrav a díkůvzdóní. Spolek Posluchaču Filosofie, Brno, 1939.

For Roman Jakobson. Essays on the Occasion of His Sixtieth Birthday, 11 October 1956. Compiled by M. Halle et al. The Hague: Mouton, 1956.

To Honor Roman Jakobson. Essays on the Occasion of His Seventieth Birthday, 11 October 1966. 3 vols. The Hague: Mouton, 1967.

Studies Presented to Professor Roman Jakobson by His Students. Edited by Ch. E. Gribble. Cambridge, Mass.: Slavica Publishers, 1968.

Poétique 2 (1971), no. 7: "Hommage à Roman Jakobson."

Critique 30 (1974), no. 322: "Roman Jakobson."

L'Arc (1975), no. 60: "Roman Jakobson."

3. *CITED WORKS BY OTHER AUTHORS*

Aginsky, B. W., and E. G. Aginsky. 1948. "The Importance of Language Universals." *Word* 4:168-172.

Barthes, Roland. 1963. "The Structuralist Activity," *Critical Essays.* Evanston: Northwestern University Press, 1972, pp. 213-220.

――――. 1964. *Elements of Semiology.* Boston: Beacon, 1970.

Benussi, Vittorio. 1913. *Psychologie der Zeitauffassung.* Heidelberg.

Berlin, Brent, and Paul Kay. 1969. *Basic Color Terms.* Berkeley: University of California Press.

Bierwisch, Manfred. 1966. *Modern Linguistics. Its Development, Method and Problems.* The Hague: Mouton, 1971.

――――. 1967a. "Some Semantic Universals of German Adjectivals." *Foundations of Language* 3:1-36.

――――. 1967b. "Skizze der generativen Phonologie." *Studia Grammatica* 6:7-33.

Bloomfield, Leonard. 1933. *Language.* New York: Henry Holt & Co.

Brentano, Franz. 1924/25. *Psychology from an Empirical Standpoint,* edited by Oskar Kraus. New York: Humanities Press, 1973.

Brøndal, Viggo. 1940. "Compensation et variation: Deux principes de linguistique générale." *Essais de linguistique générale.* Copenhagen: Munksgaard, 1943, pp. 105-116.

Bühler, Karl. 1934. *Sprachtheorie.* Stuttgart: Fischer, 1965.

Carnap, Rudolf. 1928. *The Logical Structure of the World.* Berkeley: University of California Press, 1973.

Chomsky, Noam. 1957a. *Syntactic Structures.* The Hague: Mouton.

――――. 1957b. Review of *Fundamentals of Language,* by R. Jakobson and M. Halle. *International Journal of American Linguistics* 23:234-242.

――――. 1964. *Current Issues in Linguistic Theory.* The Hague: Mouton.

――――. 1965. *Aspects of the Theory of Syntax.* Cambridge, Mass.: M.I.T. Press.

――――. 1966. *Cartesian Linguistics.* New York: Harper & Row.

――――. 1972a. *Language and Mind.* Enlarged Edition. New York: Harcourt Brace Jovanovich.

――――. 1972b. "Entretien de Noam Chomsky avec Jean Paris." In *Hypothèses,* Collection *Change.* Paris: Seghers/Laffont, pp. 63-71.

Chomsky, Noam, and Morris Halle. 1968. *The Sound Pattern of English.* New York: Harper & Row.

Clark, Herbert H. 1970. "The Primitive Nature of Children's Relational Concepts." In *Cognition and the Development of Language,* edited by John R. Hayes. New York: Wiley, pp. 269-278.

———. 1973. "Space, Time, Semantics, and the Child." In *Cognitive Development and the Acquisition of Language,* edited by Timothy E. Moore. New York: Academic Press, pp. 27-63.

CLP (*Cercle linguistique de Prague*). 1929. "Thèses (proposées au Premier congrès des philologues slaves)." *Travaux du Cercle linguistique de Prague* 1:7-29.

———. 1931a. "Réunion phonologique internationale tenue à Prague: Procèsverbeaux des séances du 18 au 21 décembre 1930." *Travaux du Cercle linguistique de Prague* 4:289-305.

———. 1931b. "Projet de terminologie phonologique standardisée." *Travaux du Cercle linguistique de Prague* 4:309-326.

Cohen, Rudolf; Peter Hartmann; Dorothea Engel; Stephanie Kelter; Gudula List; and Hans Strohner. 1975. *Experimentalpsychologische Untersuchungen zur linguistischen Erfassung aphatischer Störungen.* Dritter Bericht an die Deutsche Forschungsgemeinschaft. Constance: Universität, Fachbereich Psychologie.

Delattre, Pierre. 1968. "From Acoustic Cues to Distinctive Features." *Phonetica* 18:198-230.

Delbrück, Berthold. 1882. *Introduction to the Study of Language.* Leipzig: Breitkopf and Härtel.

De Mauro, Tullio. 1972. "Notes biographiques et critiques sur F. de Saussure." In Saussure, Ferdinand de, *Cours de linguistique générale,* edited by Tullio De Mauro. Paris: Payot, pp. 319-495.

Derrida, Jacques. 1967. *De la grammatologie.* Paris: Minuit.

———. 1968. "Sémiologie et grammatologie." *Information sur les sciences sociales* 7 (3):135-148.

Derwing, Bruce L. 1973. *Transformational Grammar as a Theory of Language Acquisition.* Cambridge: Cambridge University Press.

Dilthey, Wilhelm. 1894. "Ideen über eine beschreibende und zergliedernde Psychologie." *Gesammelte Schriften.* Vol. 5. Stuttgart: Teubner, 1957, pp. 139-240.

Ehrenfels, Christian von. 1890. "Über 'Gestaltqualitäten.' " *Vierteljahrsschrift für wissenschaftliche Philosophie* 14:249-292.

Engler, Rudolf. 1970. "Semiologische Lese (Betrachtungen zu Saussure, Salviati und Chrétien de Troyes)." In *Linguistique contemporaine. Hommage à Eric Buyssens.* Brussels: Ed. de l'Institut de Sociologie, pp. 61-73.

Engliš, Karel. 1930. *Begründung der Teleologie als Form des empirischen Erkennens.* Brno.

Foucault, Michel. 1966. "Entretien avec Michel Foucault" (by Madeleine Chapsal). *La Quinzaine littéraire,* May 15, 1966, no. 5:14-15.

Frege, Gottlob. 1892. "On Sense and Nominatum." In *Readings in Philosophical Analysis,* edited by Herbert Feigl and Wilfrid Sellars. New York: Appleton-Century-Crofts, 1949, pp. 85-102.

Freud, Sigmund. 1900. *The Interpretation of Dreams.* Vols. 4 and 5 of *The Complete Psychological Works.* London: Hogarth, 1953.

————. 1916/17. *Introductory Lectures on Psycho-Analysis.* Vols. 1-16 of *The Complete Psychological Works.* London: Hogarth, 1963.

Genette, Gérard. 1970. "Métonymie chez Proust ou la naissance du Récit." *Poétique* 1/2(1970):156-173.

Goodglass, Harold, and J. Hunt. 1958. "Grammatical Complexity and Aphasic Speech." *Word* 14:197-207.

Greenberg, Joseph H. 1959. Review of *Fundamentals of Language,* by R. Jakobson and M. Halle. *American Anthropologist* 61:157-158.

————, ed. 1963. *Universals of Language.* Cambridge, Mass.: M.I.T. Press.

————. 1966. *Language Universals.* The Hague: Mouton.

Gurwitsch, Aron. 1935. "Psychologie du langage." *Revue philosophique de la France et de l'étranger* 120:399-439.

Heidegger, Martin. 1927. *Being and Time.* London: SCM Press, 1962.

Herbart, Johann F. 1824. *Psychologie als Wissenschaft* I. Vol. 5 of *Sämtliche Werke.* Langensalza, 1890.

Hjelmslev, Louis. 1943. *Prolegomena to a Theory of Language.* Bloomington: Indiana University Press, 1953.

Hockett, Charles F. 1954. "Two Models of Grammatical Description." *Word* 10:210-234.

Holenstein, Elmar. 1972. *Phänomenologie der Assoziation.* The Hague: Nijhoff.

————. 1973. "Jakobson and Husserl: A Contribution to the Genealogy of Structuralism." 2nd, rev. version. *The Human Context* 7/1 (1975):61-83.

_____. 1974a. "A New Essay Concerning the Basic Relations of Language." *Semiotica* 12:97-128.

_____. 1974b. "Die Grenzen der phänomenologischen Reduktion der Phonologie oder Eine strukturalistische Lektion in Phänomenologie." *Phänomenologische Studien* 2. Freiburg: Alber, forthcoming.

Hume, David. 1777. *An Enquiry concerning Human Understanding: Enquiries concerning the Human Understanding and concerning the Principles of Morals.* Edited by L. A. Selby-Bigge. Oxford: Clarendon, 1970.

Husserl, Edmund. 1882. "Beiträge zur Variationsrechnung." Dissertation, Vienna. Manuscript in the archives of the University of Vienna, copy in the Husserl-Archives in Louvain, Belgium.

_____. 1913. *Logical Investigations.* New York: Humanities Press, 1970.

_____. 1928/1966. *Zur Phänomenologie des inneren Zeitbewusstseins* (1893-1917). Vol. 10 of *Husserliana.* The Hague: Nijhoff, 1966. Partial English translation: *The Phenomenology of Internal Time-Consciousness.* Bloomington: Indiana University Press, 1964.

_____. 1931. *Cartesian Meditations.* The Hague: Nijhoff, 1960.

_____. 1939. *Experience and Judgment.* Evanston: Northwestern University Press, 1973.

Ivić, Pavle. 1965. "Roman Jakobson and the Growth of Phonology." *Linguistics* 18:35-78.

Joos, Martin. 1957. Review of *Fundamentals of Language,* by R. Jakobson and M. Halle. *Language* 33:408-415.

Klein, Felix. 1872. "Das Erlanger Programm (Vergleichende Betrachtungen über neuere geometrische Forschungen)." *Gesammelte mathematische Abhandlungen.* Vol. 1. Berlin, 1921, pp. 460-497.

Koffka, Kurt. 1912. *Zur Analyse der Vorstellungen und ihrer Gesetze.* Leipzig.

Kruszewski, N. (Mikołaj). 1884ff. "Prinzipien der Sprachentwicklung." *Internationale Zeitschrift für allgemeine Sprachwissenschaft* 1:295-307; 2:258-268; 3:145-187; 5:339-360.

Lacan, Jacques. 1957. "L'instance de la lettre dans l'inconscient ou la raison depuis Freud." *Ecrits.* Paris: Seuil, 1966, pp. 493-528.

Lévi-Strauss, Claude. 1950. "Introduction à l'oeuvre de Marcel Mauss." In Mauss, Marcel, *Sociologie et anthropologie.* Paris: Presses

Universitaires de France, pp. IX-LII.

―――. 1962. *The Savage Mind.* Chicago: University of Chicago Press, 1966.

―――. 1963. "Réponses à quelques questions." *Esprit* 31, 628-653.

―――. 1964. *The Raw and the Cooked.* Vol. 1 of *Introduction to a Science of Mythology.* New York: Harper & Row, 1969.

―――. 1965. "Le triangle culinaire." *L'Arc* 26:19-29.

―――. 1968. *L'Origine des manières de table.* Vol. 3 of *Mythologiques.* Paris: Plon.

―――. 1973a. "Structuralism and Ecology." *Social Science Information* 12/1:7-23.

―――. 1973b. "Un entretien avec Claude Lévi-Strauss" (by Lucien Malson). *Le Monde,* December 8, 1973.

Lewin, Kurt. 1926. "Untersuchungen zur Handlungs— und Affektpsychologie." *Psychologische Forschung* 7:294-385.

Luria, A. R. 1973. "Two Basic Kinds of Aphasic Disorders." *Linguistics,* 115:57-66.

Martinet, André. 1960. *Elements of General Linguistics.* Chicago: University of Chicago Press, 1964.

Marty, Anton. 1875. *Über den Ursprung der Sprache.* Würzburg.

―――. 1879. *Die Frage nach der geschichtlichen Entwicklung des Farbensinns.* Vienna.

―――. 1884ff., "Über subjektlose Sätze und das Verhältnis der Grammatik zu Logik und Psychologie." In *Gesammelte Schriften,* vol. 2, part 1. Halle: Niemeyer, 1918, pp. 3-364.

―――. 1908. *Untersuchungen zur Grundlegung der allgemeinen Grammatik und Sprachphilosophie.* vol. 1. Halle: Niemeyer.

Masaryk, Thomas G. 1887. *Versuch einer konkreten Logik.* Vienna: Konegen.

Mathesius, Vilém. 1931a. "Discours d'ouverture. Réunion phonologique internationale tenue à Prague (du 18 au 21 décembre 1930)." *Travaux du Cercle linguistique de Prague* 4:291-293.

―――. 1931b. "La place de la linguistique fonctionelle et structurale dans le développement général des études linguistiques." *Časopis pro moderni filologii* 18:1-7.

Mukařovský, Jan. 1940. "O jazyce básnickém." *Kapitoly z české poetiky.* Vol. 1. Prague, 1948, pp. 78-128.

Naef, Adolf. 1919. *Idealistische Morphologie und Phylogenetik.* Jena:

Fischer.

Odum, Eugene P. 1971. *Fundamentals of Ecology.* 3rd ed. Philadelphia: Saunders.

Osthoff, Hermann. 1879. *Das physiologische und psychologische Moment in der sprachlichen Formenbildung.* Berlin: Habel.

Osthoff, Hermann, and Karl Brugman(n). 1878. "Preface to Morphological Investigations in the Sphere of the Indo-European Languages I." In *A Reader in Nineteenth-Century Historical Indo-European Linguistics,* edited by Winfried P. Lehmann. Bloomington: Indiana University Press, 1967, pp. 197-209.

Parret, Herman. 1974. *Discussing Language.* The Hague: Mouton.

Paul, Hermann. 1889. *Principles of the History of Language.* New York: Macmillan. Fallacious translation of *Prinzipien der Sprachgeschichte*; cf. 7th ed., Tübingen: Niemeyer, 1966.

Pike, Kenneth L. 1967. *Language in Relation to a Unified Theory of the Structure of Human Behavior.* 2nd rev. ed. The Hague: Mouton.

Pinborg, Jan. 1967. *Die Entwicklung der Sprachtheorie im Mittelalter.* Münster: Aschendorff.

Pingaud, Bernard. 1965. "Comment on devient structuraliste?" *L'Arc* 26:1-5.

Pomorska, Krystyna. 1968. *Russian Formalist Theory and its Poetic Ambiance.* The Hague: Mouton.

Pos, Hendrik J. 1938. "La notion d'opposition en linguistique." In *Onzième congrès international de psychologie, Paris, 1937.* Paris: Alcan, pp. 246-247.

_____. 1939a. "Perspectives du structuralisme." *Travaux du Cercle linguistique de Prague* 8:71-78.

_____. 1939b. "Phénoménologie et linguistique." *Revue internationale de philosophie* 1:354-365.

Putschke, Wolfgang. 1969. "Zur forschungsgeschichtlichen Stellung der junggrammatischen Schule." *Zeitschrift für Dialektologie und Linguistik* 36:19-48.

Quine, Willard Van Orman. 1960. *Word and Object.* Cambridge, Mass.: M.I.T. Press.

Reiter, Josef. 1970. "Struktur und Geschichte." *Zeitschrift für philosophische Forschung* 24:159-182.

Ricoeur, Paul. 1963. "Structure and Hermeneutics." In *The Conflict of*

Interpretations. Evanston: Northwestern University Press, 1974, pp. 27-61.

———. 1969. "The Question of the Subject: The Challenge of Semiology." In *The Conflict of Interpretations.* Evanston: Northwestern University Press, 1974, pp. 236-266.

Risset, Jacqueline. 1971. "Théorie et fascination." In *Paragone.* Florence, pp. 30-52.

Russell, Bertrand. 1919. *Introduction to Mathematical Philosophy.* London: Allan & Unwin.

Sangster, Rodney B. 1970. *The Linguistic Thought of Roman Jakobson.* Ann Arbor: University Microfilms.

Sapir, Edward. 1921. *Language.* New York: Harcourt, Brace & World.

———. 1933. "The Psychological Reality of Phonemes." *Selected Writings.* Berkeley: University of California Press, 1963, pp. 46-60.

Sartre, Jean-Paul. 1943. *Being and Nothingness.* New York: Philosophical Library, 1956.

———. 1966. "Jean-Paul Sartre répond: Entretien avec Bernard Pingaud." *L'Arc* 30:87-96.

Saussure, Ferdinand de. 1916. *Course in General Linguistics.* New York: McGraw-Hill, 1966.

———. 1967ff. *Cours de linguistique générale.* Critical edition by Rudolf Engler. Wiesbaden: Harrassowitz.

Simpson, George G. 1964. "The Meaning of Taxonomic Statements." In *Classification and Human Evolution,* edited by Sherwood L. Washburn. London: Methuen, pp. 1-31.

Sokal, Robert R., and Peter H. A. Sneath. 1963. *Principles of Numerical Taxonomy.* San Francisco/London: Freeman.

Spiegelberg, Herbert. 1971. "From Husserl to Heidegger. Excerpts from a 1928 Freiburg Diary by W. R. Boyce Gibson." *The Journal of the British Society for Phenomenology* 2:58-82.

Steiner, Peter, and Wendy Steiner. 1976. "The Relational Axes of Poetic Language." Postscript to Jan Mukařovský, *On Poetic Language.* Lisse: De Ridder Press, pp. 71-86.

Steinthal, Heymann. 1871. *Abriss der Sprachwissenschaft.* Vol. 1. Berlin.

Stumpf, Carl. 1907. "Zur Einteilung der Wissenschaften." In *Abhandlungen der Königlich Preussischen Akademie der Wissenschaften vom Jahre 1906.* Berlin.

Titchener, Edward B. 1898. "The Postulates of a Structural Psychology." *The Philosophical Review* 7:449-465.

Trubetzkoy, Nikolaj S. 1920. *Evropa i Čelovečestvo.* Sofia. German translation: *Europa und die Menschheit.* Munich, 1922.

———. 1929. "Sur la 'morphonologie.' " *Travaux du Cercle linguistique de Prague* 1:85-88.

———. 1931. "Die phonologischen Systeme." *Travaux du Cercle linguistique de Prague* 4:96-116.

———. 1933. "La phonologie actuelle." *Journal de psychologie* 30:227-246.

———. 1939. *Grundzüge der Phonologie. Travaux du Cercle linguistique de Prague* 7, Reprint: Göttingen: Vandenhoek & Ruprecht. 5th ed. 1971.

Tschiževskij (Čiževskij), Dmitrij. 1961. *Hegel bei den Slaven.* 2nd ed. Darmstadt: Wissenschaftliche Buchgesellschaft.

Ungeheuer, Gerold. 1959. "Das logistische Fundament binärer Phonemklassifikationen." *Studia Linguistica* 13:67-97.

Vallier, Dora. 1975. "Malevitch et le modèle linguistique en peinture." *Critique* 334:284-296.

Wallon, Henri. 1945. *Les origines de la pensée chez l'enfant.* Vol. 1. Paris: Presses Universitaires de France.

Weigl, Egon, and Manfred Bierwisch. 1970. "Neuropsychology and Linguistics: Topics of Common Research." *Foundations of Language* 6:1-18.

Winteler, Jost. 1876. *Die Kerenzer Mundart des Kantons Glarus in ihren Grundzügen dargestellt.* Leipzig/Heidelberg: Winter.

Wittgenstein, Ludwig. 1968. *Philosophische Untersuchungen/ Philosophical Investigations.* Oxford: Blackwell.

INDEX OF NAMES

INDEX OF SUBJECTS